Pay No Attention
to that Man Behind the Curtain

Also by Patrick Griffin

Losing Patients:
The Challenge of Modern Hospital Marketing (forthcoming)

Also by Kevin Flynn

Wicked Intentions:
A Remote Farmhouse, a Beautiful Temptress,
and the Lovers She Murdered

Our Little Secret:
The True Story of a Teenager Killer and the Silence
of a Small New England Town

Pay No Attention
to that Man Behind the Curtain

How technology has made traditional advertising obsolete

BY

PATRICK GRIFFIN

WITH

KEVIN FLYNN

FOREWORD BY MIKE MURPHY

iUniverse, Inc.
New York   Bloomington

Copyright © 2010 by GY&K

All rights reserved. No part of this book may be used or reproduced by any means, graphic, electronic, or mechanical, including photocopying, recording, taping or by any information storage retrieval system without the written permission of the publisher except in the case of brief quotations embodied in critical articles and reviews.

iUniverse books may be ordered through booksellers or by contacting:

iUniverse
1663 Liberty Drive
Bloomington, IN 47403
www.iuniverse.com
1-800-Authors (1-800-288-4677)

Because of the dynamic nature of the Internet, any Web addresses or links contained in this book may have changed since publication and may no longer be valid. The views expressed in this work are solely those of the author and do not necessarily reflect the views of the publisher, and the publisher hereby disclaims any responsibility for them.

ISBN: 978-1-4502-1947-1 (sc)
ISBN: 978-1-4502-1949-5 (hc)
ISBN: 978-1-4502-1948-8 (ebook)

Printed in the United States of America

iUniverse rev. date: 04/19/2010

To Sally, Justin and Tyler:
"on whose constant intercession I rely for help."

- PWG

Author's note

This book uses the words and actions of others to illustrate points which are factual as I know them to have occurred. Where dialogue attributed to an actual individual appears within quotation marks, it comes from that speaker and has been reconstructed as said to the best of my knowledge. Where dialogue is not in quotation marks, or is otherwise indirectly quoted, it has been paraphrased, reflecting only a lack of certainty about the precise wording used by the individual and not the nature, intention, or tone of the statement.

Foreword

Screw Tolstoy. Read Griffin.

There. I got your attention with four words of punchy copy. After all, this is the foreword to a book about advertising. And since my end of the ad racket is political advertising, I figured I would start off with a nice punchy bit of political style ad copy: short, direct, negative... and patently untrue.

You should read Tolstoy. But read Griffin first. More pictures.

I first met Pat Griffin in 1992 when the Bush re-election High Command needed an idiot, namely me, to go to New Hampshire and shoot a package of man-on-the-street spots for the President's re-election. Pat Buchanan was setting the Granite State on fire and the brass thought we'd need some spots to make sure nothing awful happened in New Hampshire's famously, um, quirky primaries. They assured me that a savvy local ad guy would be there to make sure it all went smoothly.

As you will soon read, I met Pat at a dreary shopping center somewhere in suburban Manchester. According to the official legends of the glorious 1988 Bush campaign, we had arrived at a Holy Place where mobs of happy voters had once fought for the chance to jump in front of a campaign team camera and say wonderful things about George H.W. Bush. All we had to do is turn on the camera and capture the magic again.

I knew we might be in trouble when I noticed Pat frequently glancing back at our van. He'd kept the engine running.

We fired up the camera and started stopping voters, asking them about the President. My memory goes a bit dim after that. (They say this happens to survivors of plane crashes too.) There was shouting. Maybe a large knife, or cleaver. I don't think there were gunshots, but it is hard to remember. Let's just say it didn't go well at all. I do remember Pat's distinctive Irish Happy Warrior laugh and maybe the squealing of van tires as we ultimately made our escape.

Later that day in the first of what turned out to be many gallows humor-drenched meals with Pat, he explained to me what he'd been telling the Bush campaign leadership back in Washington DC for months, to no avail. The Prez was in trouble. The Buchanan movement was about much more than the candidate hollering screeds about the Red Chinese to a bunch of shivering guys dressed in Colonial garb standing in front of closed down shoe factories on snowy street corners in Manchester's Millyard. Buchanan was only the tip of the iceberg. It was actually the early manifestation of far deeper and more powerful forces simmering in the Granite State and beyond that if not checked and dealt with frankly, would cost the President not just New Hampshire but the entire election. Pat Griffin didn't need a poll to see the future because Pat has a natural feel for the music of politics. The rhythm of it. I think it is because Pat is a natural salesman. He understands what selling is, in advertising, in politics, and in life. That has given him an old-school adman's golden gut with a clear understanding of the most technologically savvy way to deploy key messages to the masses.

Pat made such an impression on me that I made it a point to try to drag him into every campaign that took me anywhere near New England. He had a knack for seeing through the clutter and understanding the type of adverting that breaks though. He understands positioning strategy. Most of all, he knew that when you sell a candidate you deal with people on a uniquely human level. First you must try to understand the candidate's point of view as they get shoved into the Bizarro Land universe of being sold like a product. You have to keep in mind that the voters don't see candidates as products at all, but instead as people, whom they size up with all the primal tools of the animal kingdom. Every glance, tic, and general peculiarity is glared at through a tough filtering microscope that expects the worst. Somehow out of that cloud of neurosis a candidate's image is created.

You should pay attention to what Pat says in this book about technology and why it's changing the way we market. Each day, more devices come out that change fundamentally the way consumers interact with content. Whether it's the Kindle or the iPad, or the promise of 3D HD television in every home, we're all going to be using media differently in the future. And the digital future is now.

Which means whether you sell chewing gum or lipstick (or in my case – political candidates), you now have a chance to see what works with your customers and what doesn't. The technology we have today allows us to count exactly how many people click on and read a banner ad – not just guess how many might have read it based on an everdwindling newspaper circulation audit. In *Pay No Attention to that Man Behind the Curtain,* Pat's going to let you in on a secret: those people who actually read that banner ad are much more inclined to buy your product than the person who browses by it. They're signaling themselves as interested, and better yet, ready to *buy in*. It's not just about awareness and perception. It's about bringing that consumer closer to the product (gum, lipstick, or maybe the next President).

Pat might have cut his teeth in the heady days of TV advertising, when agencies were printing their own money, but he's not stuck there. Pat has embraced the way we all use media and its implications on advertising. He calls himself "media agnostic," meaning he's not married to any one medium and will give you an honest assessment of which platforms are likely to work for your product or service. And which will not. Imagine that! Who says you can't teach old dogs new tricks?

One reason I think Pat is so good at navigating all this is that he notices things other people miss. Pat is an accomplished mimic and he has that strange savant genius-like ability to zoom in on somebody and play back the person's exact vibe, usually in a very, very funny way. He gets to the truth of it, with uncanny precision.

All of which is why I'm glad Pat wrote this book. If you have to read one book on advertising, well, read Ogilvy's. But then read Pat's book second. *Pay No Attention to that Man Behind the Curtain* is a wonderful look at what makes some advertising great and some utterly useless. It is very funny, opinionated, and dead-on correct. Most of all, it is streetwise. This is a book built on the combination of intelligence and experience. That makes it very useful. You will learn a lot about advertising from *Pay No Attention* and despite the painfully funny stories of dumb decisions, foolhardy candidates, and cement headed clients, this advertising thing can be one very interesting, exciting, and – yes – even rewarding way to make a living.

Especially so if you get to work with a gifted, talented, and happy soul like Pat Griffin along the way. I know it was that way for me.

Mike Murphy
Los Angeles, California
May 2010

Acknowledgement

Everyone has a book in them. Maybe two or three. I knew I had one and I began to realize at the age of 50 that it was time to at least put some of my thoughts, ideas, life experiences, and moving violations in the advertising business on paper. It was apparent to me that the time had come to write a book based on a couple of other key factors as well. First: when you begin your manuscript and the autobiographical sections include references to a lot of people you have encountered which are preceded by the term "the late," it's time to write a book. Second, I cannot think of a business that has undergone as much change as the business of marketing communications. Today even though our business model has changed drastically in these last years (months, weeks, days, hours) the advertising business has largely been unwilling – or worse – unable to adopt the changes necessary to survive and thrive in this new paradigm.

If you're picking up this book looking for an instruction manual on how to "do" advertising, don't look here. I'm no David Ogilvy and I'm not trying to be. This is not that kind of book. While I offer answers to many modern marketing problems, there are more questions to be addressed than anyone can confidently write about. I can tell you I've seen many things change in this industry (and things will continue to change). What I can comment on is the absurdity of waste found in the system, waste that grows exponentially when advertising executives fail to recognize the grand shift in our traditional media habits. What you will find in this book is that a lot of what I've learned, I learned the hard way. It's true what George Santayana said: "Those who cannot learn from history are doomed to repeat it."

This as we have all been told is "the age of convergence" and much of what you read in this book – especially regarding technology – you may already know. If you don't know, then read fast, because frankly this book is sadly already obsolete!

Since this tome went to press the world will have changed in more ways than even the highest paid "Futurist" can begin to imagine. That's okay because at the very least these chapters will reflect the history of "what was" just before the presses rolled. So when it comes to cutting edge and the new paradigm, you might find this volume tucked in the "Recent History" or "Semi-Current Events" sections of your local bookseller or online.

The advertising business as I once knew it has gone the way of the local blacksmith from days of yore. It remains exciting and vibrant and in spite of the new ways we disseminate content, creativity remains the one attribute of connecting with consumers that in my estimation will never change. The way we channel that creativity and the consumer's role in the process of accepting, processing, and hopefully adopting products, services, institutions, politicians, and (although I hate the word) "brands" remains in a state of constant flux. For that I blame Steve Jobs.

Content is King! But exporting content, now that's the trick. So many people who practice "advertising" today simply don't get this – they never will. This is why the number of advertising agencies and practitioners of the Dark Arts of Advertising will also continue to follow the blacksmith and the T-rex on the road to irrelevance. How then to monetize content on the web? How can we convince customers to opt in and become raving fans of a product thereby spreading the word of a product's value and virtue far more credibly than Mr. Whipple or The Juice Man?

To quote Arun Sundararajan, an Associate Professor of Information and Operations and Management Sciences at NYU, the future of all marketing communications changes unilaterally with the onslaught of the consumer's network validation among peers and the technology used to virtually spread the word:

Future Marketing will be more about technology and sociology, and less about reach and communication. Strategy will shift from directly influencing consumers to mediating the influence consumers will have on each other. Under this new paradigm defined by widespread adoption of online social networking and a growing reliance on user generated content, consumers' choices and opinions become more transparent while their views, decisions, and interests shape the behavior of friends, both real and virtual. Brands will be challenged to move beyond their traditional boundaries and find a place in this vital social equation-perhaps by interactively creating a quality experience enjoyed and most important, shared by engaged consumers.

I have attempted to address this ideology throughout these pages, to offer some conclusions and leave many more to the reader. In many cases the answers are too complex for a guy like me with a liberal arts education to articulate.

So read fast and then log onto thatmanbehindthecurtain.com and watch as we update much of what has been initially written here. Add your comments, ideas, and even your disagreements. As students of relevance as well as digital citizens, your thoughts on evolving creative and technological developments, changes in media in all of its forms, and our tolerance to participate in "consuming," will continue to evolve like advertising itself. If you're a savvy consumer and you understand all the choices before you, you can add more to an on-going discussion of this book for years to come.

Everyone who writes a book always has to "acknowledge" certain people. I have always found this self-serving and somewhat annoying and have rarely bothered to read whose ass the author wishes to kiss. I have however after going through this process realized that the good luck and good fortune I have experienced in the advertising business would simply not have been possible without the formative experiences and individuals I encountered along the way. Further, that book I said we all have in us when I first started my acknowledgement rant is simply not possible without the help and support of some really talented, dedicated, and creative people. In my case most of them are my colleagues at Griffin York & Krause, which is a further indication of my good fortune to collaborate with them every day.

Book first: I did not write this tome alone. My collaborator Kevin Flynn works in our PR shop here at GY&K and is an accomplished former reporter, writer, and author of a number of books. Kevin helped me to keep my eye on this project (in spite of my hectic schedule) and helped organize my thoughts, experiences, and ideas regarding why the advertising and PR I practiced for so many years has become obsolete. Kevin helped me to find my voice and is among a select few who understands, encourages, and can communicate my dry, often cynical, sense of humor. Without Kevin's help and that of my assistant, Tina Yanuszewski, and my proofreaders Nate Grimes and Holly Cirillo, quite frankly I wouldn't have been able to complete this project – much less meet my deadlines.

My wife Sally who is my "editor in life" also provided great insight and never hesitated to tell me, "You can't use that word in this book." In addition Sally's recollection of our journey together and her unique view into how I address our journey here have provided both guidance and insight in what appears on each and every printed page.

To my colleagues at GY&K, I cannot think of a better group of professionals with whom to weather nearly 30 years in this business. So many of my team has been with me for all of my time here (some even pre-date me). These talented folks have made our company successful, our clients a lot of money, and my life (most days) a whole lot easier. I cannot thank them enough for their loyalty, friendship, professionalism, and support.

With regard to actually winding up in the business formerly known as "advertising," I have more people to thank than an Academy Award recipient, so I am going to give it a shot: My Mom and Dad are the best and for everything they have done for me, I will always be grateful. Sally, J.P., and Tyler are supportive and contributing factors in my quest to always try to better understand where this journey will ultimately lead, and the things that are really important in life. Special thanks to Bob Montgomery and his late wife, Marge, who together inspired me to believe that the business of advertising was both noble and commendable (it was also easier than becoming a rock star, actor, or Heisman Trophy Winner). Thanks to the many mentors I have had the good fortune to learn from over these many years, many of whom you will read about in the pages that follow – especially my former colleagues and friends from the Anheuser-Busch days who made me understand that the really important thing in increasing sales and market share still comes from the sales part, the human relations part. For this reason I now understand more fully why A-B used the internal slogan "Making Friends is Our Business."

To the many clients I have had the distinct privilege to work with over the years, I can honestly say that your believing in the things we created together has made every day rewarding and important.

If you like this book, let someone in your own personal network know about it. You can text it or tweet it, email it or post it on your Facebook, MySpace, or LinkedIn account. Then again, the next time you actually speak to someone (face to face) or from your handheld mobile device, just tell them about it. I would appreciate it – even though personal human contact is so *yesterday*!

Contents

Author's note	vii
Foreword	ix
Acknowledgement	xiii
A Horse of a Different Color	1
Our (Brave) New World	13
Is Your Ad Agency Extinct?	25
Dumb People Don't Make Things Any Easier	37
I Always Wanted the Job Spielberg Has	49
P.T. Barnum Had it Right	61
My Content on My Terms	73
Opting Out	85
Branding Should Only Happen to Cattle	95
Get Them Out of Here, They're Celebrities	107
Of Doughnuts, Beer, Soda & Republicans	125
So Now What?	149
Afterword	169
Index	181

"How can I help being a humbug," he said, "when all these people make me do things that everybody knows can't be done?"

The Wonderful Wizard of Oz - L. Frank Baum

Chapter one

A Horse of a Different Color

Why advertising as we've known it sucks

"No one gets in to see the Wizard," said the man in the funny green coat and handlebar mustache. "Not nobody, not no how!" The motley group assembled outside the giant doors to the Emerald City would not be turned back. They knocked again (the sign on the door read "Bell out of order, please knock") and sweet talked their way in by dropping some names and flashing a little bling.

Inside the fantastic lair of green smoke, magical sparks, and sonorous pronouncements, the mysterious figure declared, "The Beneficent Oz has every intention of granting your requests." But at a cost! A steep price must be paid. Surprisingly, the group found the resources and paid the wage. To their dismay, the mysterious figure refused to give them what they actually wanted and told them instead to come back tomorrow.

"You ungrateful creatures!" he roared. "Think yourselves lucky that I'm giving you an audience tomorrow, instead of twenty years from now! Oh! The Great Oz has spoken!"

Since before Dorothy dropped a house on the WWotE, advertisers have been promising their clients they can do all sorts of wondrous things, using what my Dad still refers to as "blue smoke and mirrors." They promise the client to give them brains, provide them courage, even make them appear to have a heart. Some of it is – as the Wizard admitted – humbug. For as the 1970s soft rock superband "America"

1

sang, "Oz never did give nothing to the Tin Man that he couldn't get from Bill Cosby or Sir Galahad*."

Like the mere mortal the Great Oz ultimately turns out to be, too often the wizards of advertising implore their clients to spend fortunes on antiquated methods that sell nothing to nobody, no way, no how. When it comes to measurable results, they tell their clients to "pay no attention to that man behind the curtain." Not because there's no magic – but because they have no way to prove to the people who pay for the ads that there is. They don't measure. They don't audit. They simply proclaim themselves wizards, provide you with a scrap of paper, and expect you to blurt out, "The sum of the square roots of any two sides of an isosceles triangle is equal to the square root of the remaining side."

Today, traditional advertising is a square peg in a society that has evolved into a round hole. You can still market your business or your product effectively – but if you only had a brain you wouldn't continue to advertise the way they did when Judy Garland popped her last Seconal. What is needed for advertisers, for business owners, and for consumers is a new way of looking at things. They need a horse of a different color.

Advertising sucks

There, I said it. *Advertising sucks.* Yes, I know I'm biting the hand that's fed me for nearly 30 years. I've spent many years and made a lot of money in advertising. I've shot countless TV commercials. I've spent more hours than I can remember in broadcast studios editing and re-editing voice-over scripts, often times desperately attempting to jam 67 seconds of copy into a 60 second spot. I've signed off on more layouts for print ads and coupon fliers than any one individual should

---

* Would you at this juncture in our book, dear reader, indulge me a parenthetical thought? In regards to America, I can totally groove out to "Sister Golden Hair," but what the hell is going on in "A Horse with No Name"? First of all, if you're out in the middle of the desert for two weeks, why not just make up a name for the horse? Secondly, how come "In the desert you can remember your name/'Cause there ain't no one for to give you no pain"? There are about five grammatical errors in that line alone. And if you have to go ride through the desert to remember your own name, you have no business taking care of a horse. Turn around and ride back to the Alzheimer's treatment facility.

be subjected to by law. I've stood in pitch meeting after pitch meeting imploring CEOs to entrust me with the good name of their brands, then told them later that (in all candor) their products weren't that good to begin with. I've made those attack ads for politicians that will – if there's any sense of justice in the world – surely relegate me to one of the farthest levels of Dante's Inferno when I die[*]. I've also logged an infinite number of hours on campaign buses to nowhere and fielded more than one middle-of-the-night phone call from a candidate's wife complaining angrily that he "doesn't have his pillow."

Advertising doesn't suck because it's a hard job. It's not. Coal mining? Now *that's* a hard job. Corrections officer? Teaching high school? Media spokesman for a Third-World dictator? All those things are way tougher than working in advertising. How do I know? Just watch TV. On "Rescue Me" all the firefighters are constantly escaping death, jumping out of windows, or are haunted by the demons of the horrors they've witnessed. On "The Shield" all the police officers regularly escape death, jumping out of windows, or are haunted by the demons of the horrors they've witnessed. On "Hannah Montana," all the high school kids are forever escaping death, jumping out of windows, or are haunted by the oily condition of their skin.[†] What happens on "Mad Men," the AMC drama about 1960s ad executives? They sit around in vintage suits on comfortable furniture smoking and drinking *all day long*. Nobody is cheating death. Nobody is jumping out windows (except in the opening credits). Nobody is haunted (except perhaps by cirrhosis of the liver or a hacking smoker's cough).

Advertising sucks because generally speaking it's no good. It's no longer effective. It's just as dated as Don Draper's suits or the community ash tray on the Sterling Cooper conference room table. So pour yourself a highball, light up a Lucky Strike, and let me tell you what I mean when I say advertising sucks.

---

[*] At least, that's what my wife has told me.

[†] I'll admit, "Hannah Montana" is the only high school TV show I could think of. It wasn't until later I thought of classics like "Saved by the Bell" or "Beverly Hills 90210." All the actors in those shows either wound up in rehab or on "Dancing with the Stars." There's also the teen high school drama "Degrassi," but that takes place in Canada so one can't take it seriously.

You're not the boss of me

Advertising sucks because now more than perhaps any other time consumers like to think for themselves (or like to believe that they can think for themselves). As soon as we're three or four years old, we don't want to hold Mommy's hand anymore. "I can do it on my own," we say (right before we spill the entire carton of milk by missing the cereal bowl). We want to be independent and self-sufficient. It was true when we were four and it's true now that we're adults.

Nobody wants to be told what to do, what to like, what to believe, or how to behave. Mothers-in-law have tried it for years and have gotten a bad rep[*]. Imagine a stranger coming up to you at a party and telling you that *his* favorite music is the best or that Senator Pickering is a "Washington insider" and is the guy you definitely shouldn't vote for. You'd think this party-goer was a tool and you'd politely excuse yourself to get more onion dip.

Nobody likes to be told what to think. And they certainly don't like to be told what to buy. In subtle and not-so-subtle ways, this is what modern advertising does. *Look at those cool sneakers. I'm drinking a premium beer. Who* wouldn't *want to save twenty-five percent on their long distance calling? Look at me with the Viagra!*

Brought to you by

Advertising sucks because the consuming public views it as, well, "advertising." We instantly can see through that age-old ruse known as a sales pitch. Our brains are constantly triaging the flow of information with which we are incessantly bombarded. When we're exposed to a commercial or some other form of advertising, our brain automatically sends this information to the "not important" lobe instead of the lobe where we keep stuff that we have to pay attention to and retain[†].

Remember our friend from the party? Suppose he pointed to the onion dip and said, "That's some of the best onion dip I've ever had." With that kind of testimonial, you're very likely to pick up a potato chip

---

[*] Not *my* mother-in-law, of course.

[†] Phone numbers, anniversaries, children's birthdays, baseball team line-ups, quotes from "The Godfather," the lyrics to "Paradise by the Dashboard Light."

and dive in. Now suppose for a minute, the guy who gave this ringing endorsement was also wearing a polo shirt with a logo for "Fred's Old Fashioned Onion Dip" embroidered on the front. Suppose that neatly arranged next to the dip on the kitchen table are several cans of "Fred's Old Fashioned Onion Dip." There's a banner on the kitchen wall for "Fred's" and this party guest hands you a 50 cents off coupon before you can even get your greasy fingers on a chip. You might look at this guy in the "Fred's Old Fashioned Onion Dip" shirt and say to yourself, "Wow. This guy *really* likes this stuff. Maybe too much." But more likely you're going to think, "This guy is getting paid to tell me he likes the onion dip." How much credence are you going to put into that "best I ever tasted" comment? Not much.

Advertising sucks because we've developed a sixth sense about what messages are important and entertaining and which are just "advertising." I call this the "advertising gland.*" We know when someone's talking jive. We're able to filter out what we think is a paid testimonial, which we assume is insincere, misleading, or biased.

Perhaps even more importantly – and this is good news for those of us who want desperately to sell stuff – consumers can also detect when a fellow consumer is truly, genuinely, and sincerely excited about a product or brand. Think about the first iPhone you ever saw. Was it in a store window or did somebody enthusiastically pull it from their pocket and show you all the whiz-bang features? These days "viral enthusiasm" expressed from one consumer to another is invaluable.

The advertising gland in the human brain has gotten bigger and more potent as ads and advertising techniques have gotten savvier. But, we still know when it's safe to go the bathroom when we're watching a sitcom. Because at the end of the day, it's just a commercial break.

Not now, I'm busy

Advertising sucks because people are disinterested. They're distracted. They don't have time to listen to the message because they're doing other things.

Do you own a radio (I'm not talking about an iPod. I mean a real radio)? If you're over the age of 15, then it's probably either in your car,

---

* Not an actual gland. See your doctor or pharmacist.

your alarm clock, or maybe the bathroom. How many times in the last 10 years has someone asked you what you were doing and you said, "Listening to the radio"? I'll bet…you can't remember. You probably said "I'm driving to work," "I'm taking a shower," "I'm making breakfast for the kids," or "Mmhumph, five more minutes please, zzzzzz." Virtually everybody that's listening to a radio right now is *doing something else as well*. The great news about a semi-annual tire sale is not likely to cut through the static already present in the listener's life.

Radio broadcasters have always known they were competing with their listeners' environment to get their attention. Today, we multitask so effortlessly that not even the most dominant form of media – the Sacred of Sacreds – the television, is immune (no matter how big your flat screen). A 2007 study by Park Associates found that seventy percent of people younger than thirty-four watch TV while online. In a report published the next year, nearly sixty-eight percent of all adults regularly watched TV while using a computer, according to BIGresearch. A 2008 study by Blinkx found that seventy percent of all adults in Britain go onto the Internet while watching television.[*] These figures don't even take into account the numbers of people who, while the television is on, are actually reading, napping, making popcorn, making whoopee, or searching for that damn remote control (it was right here a minute ago I swear to God!).

My time, not yours

Advertising sucks because people can select where and when they consume content. No longer do we have "Must-see TV" that we all felt we had to watch in order to get the inside jokes the next day at the office. If we missed "Must-see TV," we had no idea why our co-workers were shouting at each other, "No soup for you!" or singing "Smelly Cat." Now we can DVR the show or view it online and watch it over breakfast or even the following week.

---

[*] Of course, this IS Britain we're talking about. They've got like…what? Four channels? One of them is playing "football" highlights of Real Madrid? I think most of the adults in the UK are probably Googling the term "when are we getting some more TV channels in this country?"

There is no more "event TV." (Ok, the Winter Olympics have had pretty good viewership for NBC, but it feels like 70% of the coverage was ice dancing and pairs figure skating – enough already!) Even the Super Bowl, a quasi-national holiday built around watching TV, is not a guaranteed win for advertisers. According to Nielsen, TV ratings for the Super Bowl have been on the rise the past decade, but viewership historically plummets in the second half if the game becomes a blow-out*.

The tradition of watching the evening news is also quickly dying. I remember as a kid when my father would come home from work he'd fix himself a cocktail then sit down and watch the NBC Nightly News with John Chancellor. It was his chance to get caught up on what had happened around the world since he read his morning paper. My mother and I would join him in front of the TV. When the broadcast was over, we'd get up and have dinner. While the habit of watching the national news at 6:30 is still ingrained into many older viewers (as if you couldn't tell by the kinds of senior remedies and pharmaceutical products that populate the commercial breaks), fewer and fewer people are actually clocking in. In fact, according to the Television Bureau of Advertising, viewership of the Big 3 network evening newscasts has dropped more than twenty-five percent since 2005. Nearly nine out of every ten Americans is skipping the nightly news.

We no longer have to make an appointment to watch the news. Since CNN started the 24-hour news network in 1980, we can get caught up on world events at the top and bottom of *every* hour. With the Internet, we can get our news on demand, immediately. We also can predetermine what *kind* of news we want (health reports, local weather, libertarian politics, news about the cast of *Law and Order*) or conversely what kind of news we don't want to hear about (foreign policy, financial analysis, stories about war, anything to do with the Jacksons).

I can't believe I paid for the whole thing

Advertising sucks because advertisers waste too much money on ineffective ads. There's an old joke about a CEO who says, "I know half of my advertising is effective. I just don't know which half."

---

* I know that viewership in the second half of the Super Bowl plummets at my house if something funky is left in the chili or we run out of beer.

The people who spend this money have no measurable return on investment. Especially in broadcasting, there is no empirical way to know exactly how many people a commercial reaches.

The word "broadcasting" comes from an agricultural term. Instead of carefully sowing seeds into neat beds, a farmer might spread a handful of seeds over a wide area with a "broad cast." Some seeds would land on fertile soil; others would land among the rocks or weeds where they were unlikely to grow. The analogy is apt because the radio signals (and later television signals) constantly fall on the ears of people in their homes or cars. Considering the breadth and depth of those radio waves that originated at those red-and-white painted towers which blanket a region, there are quite literally thousands of square miles of message wasted on those without receivers and uninterested in the programming[*].

The industry has generally accepted the findings of ratings collection companies such as Arbitron and Nielsen to be their yardstick to determine audience size (which would help set advertising rates). But the dirty little secret about ratings is that they're all a guess. While some recent technologies, such as the People Meter, have made it easier to automatically document channel and time of viewing, most of the ratings have been collected the same way for decades. The rating shares and cumulative audience numbers are divined by surveying a small group of people, then extrapolating their answers over the larger population. Is it true that 10.3 million people watched Conan O'Brien's final episode of "The Tonight Show"? I don't know. But I'm pretty sure that Nielsen didn't actually ask 10.3 million people if they did.

This small sampling of participants is asked to keep diaries for one week and self-report what radio stations they heard or what TV shows they watched. I don't know about you, but when I was in school and given a weeklong assignment I didn't usually do it until the night before it was due. If most people are like me in this regard, then this Thursday night they'll be sitting at the kitchen table trying to remember which radio stations they bounced among while driving to work Monday morning.

---

[*] This was made abundantly clear in the mid-1970s when hundreds of man-hours were wasted at local radio stations waiting for a 43rd person to finally call in and win tickets to see Supertramp.

But the true Return on Investment isn't measured in how many bodies a commercial has reached. It's whether that commercial generated any sales for the advertiser. And there are few ways to gauge whether some guy bought that McDonald's hamburger because the company spent a reported $823 billion on advertising in 2008 – or whether he just really wanted some red meat fast.

Is there no hope?

Advertising *itself* doesn't suck. The way we *disseminate* advertising these days sucks. Over the years we've seen plenty of effective, creative ads in print and in broadcast. But while the paradigm of how we absorb information has changed, too little about advertising's better qualities have followed suit. In fact, if we as an industry keep advertising to the masses in a way that says we don't respect them, what we'll get is a bunch of angry consumers who simply decide to tune out.

Advertising is not "hawking" goods; it is the dissemination of content to appropriate micro-segmented markets. In this book, I hope not only to blow up the antiquated altar on which ad dollars continue to be sacrificed, but also offer a new premise for what 21st century advertising needs to be.

1. It should be brief.
Nobody has the time anymore for anything other than the headline or the bottom line. Advertisers ask customers for their money, but *advertisements* ask consumers for their time. They're asking for 30 or 60 seconds of attention on the radio. They're asking for a pause between page-turns to examine a full-color ad. They're asking you to wait before you click through to that webpage to click to this one instead.

The problem with asking for time is that, in some ways, it's more valuable than money. We'd rather pay a bill for premium TV channels than watch commercial television. We'd rather buy the TV series on DVD or Blu-ray than suffer through the live episodes with commercial breaks. We'd rather watch content on our tiny iPhone screen – presented with one commercial in the beginning – than enjoy the same content on our expensive wall-mounted HDTV's with 5.1 surround sound and a full complement of *words from our sponsor*.

The point is, because we're so busy multi-tasking and being distracted by work/the kids/the cat, the message has to be brief. The amount of time a person will spend on an advertisement (print/broadcast/online) is tied directly to the perceived value the person places on the information or content contained in the ad. In other words, as soon as they decide the ad is a waste of their time, they're done with the ad.

2. It should be entertaining.
I'm not going to ask for your money right away. I'm first going to be asking for your time. In exchange for that time – watching a TV commercial, reading a billboard, clicking through a pop-up ad – you should get something in exchange. It can be content, a giggle, or a useful piece of information. You should be rewarded for that time.

3. It needs to be engaging.
Creativity has never been lost, but too often it's been pushed to the back of the conversation. The ad is already competing with other content and external distractions. A contemporary advertisement (just like any truly good ad from the past) has to cut through the clutter, must grab someone's attention, and not let them go. It has to have "the gulp factor" which forces people to stop – even for a millisecond – to learn more.

4. The content should be relevant.
The way I sell a product to a stay-at-home mom[*] ought to be different from the way I sell a product to a business executive (or a skateboarding teen or working parents or someone from another demographic or lifestyle group). We have to figure out where we're most likely to be successful with a brand, identify it, and then deliver that content in a relevant fashion.

---

[*] Formerly, this demographic was referred to as the "housewife," but that's just so *Don Draper.*

It doesn't mean the *product* needs to be different for two people. There was a time when I worked for Anheuser-Busch – those fun-loving guys who bring us Budweiser and talking Clydesdales – that we thought the only people who bought beer were men between the legal drinking age and 35. We know today this simply isn't true. Women make up twenty-five percent of the beer market in the US, and researchers say they are much more discerning about their brew choices than their male counterparts. Advertising content about beers with fewer calories or made from fine ingredients are more likely to be effective with women than ads that highlight male-oriented activities[*].

5. It should be media agnostic.
Advertisers have to throw out everything they know. Who cares about newspapers? Who cares about radio, television, or magazines? Who cares about billboards and matchbook covers? Advertisers have to start over and take an objective look at how many eyes are watching or reading, and how many of those eyes belong to people who are really and truly in the target market for that product or service. There is a ton of waste (and there always has been).

6. It should have a measurable return on investment.
There has got to be a metric for assigning a value to advertising. An advertiser has to be able to say "I spent X, and I got Y out of it." For too long, Madison Avenue has said, "Well, we bought *this many* gross rating points and that's *this many* impressions which gives you *this amount* of exposure." We have had no quantitative way of finding out who is really watching and listening, who is paying attention. For years, we never tried to make our audience addressable.

Sure, you can invest in research, but after several months and after tens or hundreds of thousands of dollars, will you *really* know at the end of it all if you've done what you set out to do? If a number cruncher tells you, "Over two years, your

---

[*] Such as drinking beer.

brand recognition has moved the needle *this many* points," will you feel like the advertising was successful? There has to be a more direct, unfiltered way for the advertiser and the customer to begin a conversation, a dialogue – a relationship.

These are the things advertisers and the folks who create advertising content must start doing. If you're doing them today, then you don't suck. You're actually delivering your message in a way that your customers will appreciate, will understand, and – in many cases – look forward to. They will embrace the dynamic of your trying to make available your product to them (as opposed to hawking your product at them). And that changes things very much in the advertiser's favor: talking to the customer on *their* terms, not yours.

That, my friends, is a horse of a different color.

Chapter two

Our (Brave) New World

The times are a' changing

Futurist Arthur C. Clarke said, "Any sufficiently advanced technology is indistinguishable from magic." And our society evolves so quickly these days, he is correct. The lifestyle of a pilgrim who landed on Plymouth Rock in 1620 was not very different than a minuteman at Lexington in 1775. But who in 1800 would have foreseen in the next 100 years the Industrial Revolution, electricity and plumbing in homes, or the internal combustion engine? Who among those at Kitty Hawk in 1903 could have envisioned the Jet Age, the Television Age, the Atomic Age, the Space Age, or the Information Age? If you were somehow able to go back and show that Plymouth Rock pilgrim your contemporary lifestyle – the planes, the cars, the phones, the medicines, and the portable music devices – it would seem to that pilgrim that all of our technology was actually some kind of magic[*].

The span of time between "Ages" is getting compressed. Five years is the new twenty years. And what used to be five years is now eighteen months. None of us know what magical lifestyle awaits us or our grandchildren, but things continue to evolve thanks largely to technology.

You may not feel like there is a great difference in the life of a person in 2010 and a person in 2000 (or 1990 or 1970). We don't drive flying cars or wear metallic jumpsuits to work at the cloning factory. But there

---

[*] Which, if you *could* go back in time to Plymouth, would probably be some kind of weird magic. So perhaps an iPod wouldn't be the most impressive thing you could show an old pilgrim. But you get the point.

are changes (some subtle, some drastic) in the way you and I consume media and obtain information in our brave new world.

Anonymous vs. addressable

As a consumer, who am I and how am I identified? What brands lure me in? What loyalty do I have? For the most part, we have lived our consuming lives anonymously. When you or I walked into a store, we dropped down some green paper or plastic card and then walked out with a bag full of merchandise. As far as business owners were concerned, we may as well have all been wearing nylon stockings over our heads. Even if we paid with plastic, the digital trail we left was only useful to the credit card companies and INTERPOL.

These days it's not just a question of simply *buying* a product. As a consumer, you have to *engage in* the product. You have to *opt-in* to the product. You no longer have to go to a store to learn about a product or purchase it. We're eliminating traditional channels and allowing people to meet the products on their own terms. They can go online, view a video, and then build their own car. Hybrid? *Yes!* White walls? *No!* Stereo system? *Yes!* Color? *Cobalt blue, to match my eyes!*

Kids looking for colleges no longer read the view books or visit the campus; they first take a virtual tour. If they don't like the website, they cross the school off their list.

Consumers that were once anonymous are now addressable. That's because of the web. In exchange for a little demographic data (sometimes voluntarily offered, sometimes captured), we can now know where you live, your age, and what you like. We can then deploy relevant content using the millions of combinations of cross-tabbed data[*] used to identify and label the different segments of the market.

Spectators vs. participants

For decades, we have been spectators of the media we consumed. We found comfortable positions on the couch in front of the TV and

---

[*] Example: Blue-collar female sports fans age 49-60 with Labrador retrievers who want to save money on leather pants. This, I understand, is an emerging market with real promise.

just watched. We might have yelled at the umpire during a ballgame, shouted out the answers during *Jeopardy*, or danced at home to *American Bandstand*, but we were separate from the action.

Today, we are active participants. With the use of technology, we can interact with programming. We can instantly text our opinion on whether the ump got the call right. We can help game show contestants with answers or play simultaneously at home. We can download music from a popular dance show or even make a request.

As participants we can even affect the actual outcome of the programming. Shows like *American Idol, Dancing with the Stars,* and *Big Brother* all have audience participation elements, allowing viewers to vote on who should win and who should go home. We've all become editors and gatekeepers. We now find ourselves in the picture.

Individuals vs. networks

Advertisers like to have their message in front of as many eyeballs as possible. When we think about the term "audience," we don't look at it as a group. Sure, there were 105 million people who watched the last episode of *M*A*S*H* in February 1983, making it the most watched TV episode in US history. But historically we've looked at this as an audience of *individuals*. People don't usually watch television or listen to the radio in large groups; they watch it alone or with their family from the privacy of their home*.

Today individuals are not just solitary consumers of content. They are parts of networks of other individuals. They are linked together, interacting, IMing and billboarding. They're part of online communities and they're micro-blogging. This creates a new geometry, for if an advertiser can grab an individual who is part of a network, it's easier to virally penetrate the rest of the network too. Nothing sells a product like an endorsement from a friend, and that word-of-mouth type of advertising has a more immediate and effective conduit to these networks.

---

* One notable exception is prison, where there are large groups of people surrounding one television. However, most prison inmates are not presently "in the market" to make major purchases, so they're considered statistically insignificant.

The most credible thing a product can have today is an individual who emphatically sings its praises within their own network of friends, family, and colleagues. It's called "going viral." * Today, if someone likes a movie, they'll blog about it. If they had a really good sandwich from a local deli, they'll tweet about it on Twitter. They become a "raving fan," willing to show off their iPhone to everyone, or proclaim to their Facebook friends that the best part of their day is the iced latté they got at Dunkin Donuts. The raving fan will use technology to quickly evangelize the product to the others in their network with more efficiency (and at a much lower cost) than a traditional advertiser could ever deliver – and with far more credibility.

Characters vs. convenience

At one point, we had conversations. If we needed something in the business world, we had to pick up the phone and call the office down the hall or across town. When we needed information, that's how we got it. We'd use the phone to find out what time the meeting was, when the boss would be back in the office, and who in the secretarial pool had the most questionable virtue.† We did the same thing at home, writing letters or calling our friends. It became a significant thing to "reach out and touch someone."

Now we have to do it in 140 characters or less. We got used to it thanks to email – instant transmission of text, images, and other content. Now, emails aren't enough. If I can't text it, if I can't tweet it, if I can't communicate with you immediately and briefly, then I have a problem‡.

Conversation is different today. The written word, the expression of free thought, even the way we talk on the phone has been so affected by this that conversation is now about convenience. Ever notice how today when your cell phone rings the person never asks, "How are you?" They ask, "Where are you?" like you're wanted in fifty states by the FBI.

---

* This has nothing to do with catching swine flu.

† Laura says it's Susan.

‡ unless of course you're Tiger Woods and you become very proficient at texting… but that's a whole other story (See TMZ.com).

What is the quickest way for me to tell you where I am, what I'm doing, or what I'm experiencing? My *experience* is important to the world because I am a gatekeeper and you need to know what I am doing because you are in my network. My network cares about me, so I'm going to let you know.

We've even invented a whole new language to express these things quicker and more conveniently. We're not going to even bother spelling out "you" any more. We're just going to type "u." omg! r u stng dwn? Even stodgy company executives and hella-uncool parents understand what LOL means.*

Manageable vs. cluttered

Back in the good old days (*sans* the 1980s) if we wanted to know what was on television that night, we'd pick up a copy of *TV Guide*. It was small and fit nicely on everyone's coffee table right next to the bamboo coasters and the remote control. Thumb down to 8:00 pm and we'd likely have to choose from three network sitcoms and a documentary about cheese making in Iberia on public television. Then we could turn to the back page of the *TV Guide* and work on a moderately-challenging crossword puzzle.†

Today we have way more than four prime time choices, thanks to cable. We now have five broadcast networks, dozens of premium channels like HBO or Showtime, and cable networks dedicated to super-specific specialized programming, such as military history, college sports, and boxing matches from the 1970s. There's so much on TV at any given moment that *TV Guide* has gone to a full-sized magazine, added more pages, and still can't get everything in. They have a default M-F page, as if to say "Hey, you *know* 'General Hospital' is on at 3:00 every day this week! Do we really need to list it five times? Help us save a tree, dude!"

Instead of reading the week ahead to see what programs we might want to watch, we're simply using an on-screen guide to plan our next 90 minutes (As if any of us still actually sit in front of a TV screen for 90

---

* stfu

† Most used clue from 1976-2008: *One Day ___ Time (two words)*.

minutes anymore). Even with more than 200 channels of shows, sports, movies and news, we still complain that "there's nothing on."

The Internet is the greatest purveyor of sensory overload. There is no shortage of stuff to find online, brands to experience, programming and information to view, files to download or share. There is not just an abundance of content, there is an *overabundance* of content.

Ad executives used to say cable TV was "a mile wide and half an inch deep." In order to reach as many viewers as a typical network show, one had to run commercials on the news channel, the history channel, the sports channel, the old lady channel...and all the other channels that this fractured audience was watching. Well, if cable TV is a mile wide and half an inch deep, then the Internet is a piece of cellophane stretched across an area the size of South Dakota and parts of Idaho. There is no end to the number of websites one can view about animals, fantasy football, Civil War reenactments, or videos derivative of "Two Girls, One Cup."

You can put together the most nonsensical stream of words in a search engine and still find content to match. I picked three words at random: *salad, fuchsia, existentialism*. Somehow Google was able to find 1,560 websites with that combination. (Try it at home – you'll be amazed!)

The number of websites continues to grow exponentially. It's estimated there are 182 million different sites (some public, some private, some a combination of the two) and Google has indexed more than one trillion URL's, or, web addresses[*].

At one time, content was manageable. Now, the media landscape is cluttered. There is sensory overload. There is currently a sense of controlled chaos with an ever-decreasing sense of control.

Top-down vs. bottom-up

Where does public opinion come from and how is it influenced? At one point it came from "experts" and was distributed from the "top-down." They analyzed the quality of a product or explained the significance of an event. "The feel good hit of the summer!" a critic would rave about a movie. A travel guide would give a restaurant

---

[*] Oddly enough, thirty-nine percent deal with male enhancement

four stars. Seasoned political analysts would dissect the importance of a presidential speech or a new piece of legislation working its way through Congress. *Consumer Reports* would vet all kinds of store-bought products and rank them on every conceivable measure, including price, quality, or safety. The *New York Times* could kill a Broadway musical overnight with one bad review*. In all these examples, someone who was a recognized authority pronounced a judgment and more often than not that opinion was adopted by the public.

Today the driver for what makes up public consensus is less often "top down influence" as it is "bottom up influence." Instead of checking whether the guys in the balcony give a film "thumbs up," people will read online reviews written by other moviegoers at Rotten Tomatoes.com. Instead of looking for a rating from ZAGAT to find out which entrée tastes best, people read the customer comments on the restaurant's website or by finding it on an iPhone app. There are a slew of political commentators of all stripes and credentials in the blogosphere. Savvy shoppers now ignore the observations of impartial product testers and scan the online reader boards for people who need help troubleshooting their defective TV's, laptops, and Smartphones. Theater goers are already panning the show or opening weekend of a new movie on Twitter before the end of the 1st act, so the poor *NY Times* critic's review is trumped by the blogosphere before he gets a chance to kill the show himself. This was the case with the movie "Brüno," which saw its Saturday and Sunday ticket sales drop $20 million below expectations thanks to moviegoers who flamed it on Twitter. *Time* magazine said, "Brüno could be the first movie defeated by the Twitter effect." More reputations are made (and maligned) on the Internet and social media than ever before.

Stationary vs. mobile

As I said, today the new "how are you" is "where are you?"

If you have the ability to communicate wirelessly on your laptop, cell phone, or other device, you can be anywhere listening to or watching content or conducting business. The ability – nay, thy God-given right!

---

* True example: "Yours, Anne" a 1985 song and dance show about the life of Anne Frank at Playhouse 91. One of Broadway's biggest bombs, it never had a chance.

– to link in wirelessly is so ubiquitous that even the Crosier-Pearson-Mayfield Funeral Home in Burleson, Texas has a Wi-Fi connection[*].

We were used to growing up in a stationary world. There was always a wire stuck in a wall somewhere. Now with better batteries and improved technology, we've gone from a stationary world to a mobile one. We all want to be wireless. The average guy sipping a mochachino at Starbucks – texting and browsing on his laptop – is sucking in more radio frequency than the first Apollo mission. No one wants to be tethered to a wall; they'd rather be in an iron lung.

Time delay vs. real time

There are dozens of examples throughout history of the tardy deliverance of critical information. Andrew Jackson fought the Battle of New Orleans two weeks after the Treaty of Ghent ended the War of 1812[†]. It took nearly a week for news of Lincoln's assassination to travel the country. Even television reports from the Vietnam War[‡] – perceived by so many to be immediate and intimate – were in fact filmed, processed, and air-mailed several days prior to actual broadcast.

For the spread of news and information, there is no longer a time delay. We can get information – news bulletins, sports scores, weather alerts – in real time, as it's happening. Television networks can broadcast live from any corner of the globe. People are getting text messages of breaking news stories, pushing them to TV stations or websites for further coverage. Photographers can shoot a picture of a campaign speech, write a caption, and upload it before the speech is over. Sportswriters are blogging *during* the games. Geraldo Rivera actually got expelled from Iraq during the 2003 invasion because he sketched out a map of where US troops were about to travel – what a patriot!

As things move in real time, there is less time to respond and react to events. There is also little or no time for reflection (or even due diligence) about the veracity of content or the effect of publishing it. This creates even more challenges for those trying to shape a public message.

---

[*] True story. I guess it's so you can update your Facebook status to "still grieving :("

[†] Not actually in 1812.

[‡] Actually held in Vietnam

On schedule vs. on demand

There was a time when people made an appointment to watch their favorite television shows. Whether it was Ed Sullivan's "Toast of the Town" or "The Tonight Show with Johnny Carson," our ancestors made that appointment because they had no other option. They had to be in front of the TV when the show started, otherwise they'd miss it.

VCR's began the revolution of freeing us from watching prime time shows any time of day. Today, the DVR makes it infinitely simpler to record, organize, and playback the shows we missed. We can also get other content "on demand," shows and movies selected and instantly viewed. You don't even need a TV to watch your favorite shows. You can download episodes to your computer, your Smartphone, or any other number of devices.

The ability to get content on demand has altered the offerings of news departments, of television networks, and of virtually every other website. We don't even need to go to a computer to learn about breaking news. News alerts are now pushed to us by text message as they happen — severe weather bulletins, in-game score changes, video highlights, Amber alerts, lottery numbers. When all this information is being passively delivered to us, we're no longer *on demand*; we're *beyond demand*.

Advertisers pay vs. consumers pay

When broadcast programming on radio and television began, the advertiser was considered a sponsor in the truest sense of the word. Like a Renaissance patron of the arts, they provided the money to make a show possible. The audience perceived them to be partners with the network in producing the show. The Liggett & Myers Tobacco Company brought the world the "Chesterfield Supper Club." Milton Berle's show was the "Texaco Star Theater." There was the "Alcola Hour," the "20th Century Fox Hour," and the "Colgate Comedy Hour." People were urged to "See the USA in your Chevrolet" on the "Dinah Shore Chevy Show." There were even some very rudimentary forms of product placement, like all the Studebakers being driven in "Mr. Ed" or Fred Flintstone smoking Winstons.

Advertisers still sponsor network programming, but we've entered an age of paid avoidance. More than ever consumers are willing to pay a monthly fee to watch quality programming like "The Sopranos" or "Entourage" on HBO or listen to their favorite music on Sirius/XM satellite radio. They'll buy a whole season of "Desperate Housewives" on Blu-ray. They'll pay for an episode of "Heroes" from iTunes or log onto Hulu. There are other reasons for the popularity of these content streams – convenience and portability among them. It's clear that the pain threshold for many consumers is at the point where they'd rather pay for the content and avoid the advertising, than sit through a bunch of commercials. It's like the pretty girl at the end of the bar who sends back the drink the inebriated conventioneer bought for her: *no thanks, I'd rather pay for it myself.**

Left brain vs. right brain

We know there is a left brain and a right brain. The left brain is highly analytical. It's where logic rules and abstract details are comprehended and processed. It's where algebra gets figured out. It's where quantitative analysis takes place. It's very data-driven. The right side of the brain is where creativity takes place. It's where fantasy and imagination are born. It's where concepts are born, poetry is written, and where conceptual flights of fancy are taken.

In the 1950s and 1960s, there was a huge pull away from the left-brained, data-driven, market-based research that permeated most of American advertising (e.g. "Only Dove is one-quarter moisturizing cream[†]"). Then the focus was on ads that were more right-brained: creative, entertaining, and fun (e.g. Alka-Seltzer's "*Mama Mia*! That's a spicy meat-a-ball..."). At that point the culture of advertising changed and focused more on being entertaining and clever as opposed to necessarily being effective.

Advertising today sucks because we've focused only on the right-side of the brain for so long, we no longer care about results. Advertisers must be creative, but smarter. It can no longer be left brain versus right brain,

---

* Translation: "You're creepy. Leave me alone."

† As if they would have sold fewer bars of soap if it had only been 3/16 moisturizing cream.

but left brain *and* right brain together. Creativity derived from a sound strategy with real tools to measure the effectiveness of the message.

So much of today's advertising sucks because it refuses to get *ahead* of the changes in technology and lifestyle which consumers are demanding. We need a better approach because even John Smith, Pocahontas, and the rest of the gang at Plymouth knew that someday the world would change.

It has.

Chapter three

Is Your Ad Agency Extinct?

Stop marketing like it's twenty years ago

Many of the young Turks and old veterans at your friendly neighborhood advertising agency view themselves in a very romantic and stylized way. They see themselves as modern day Don Drapers from "Mad Men." The problem with Don Draper is that he is a caricature of what advertising was yesterday – not what it needs to be today or tomorrow. Even those near-extinct Madison Avenue types imagine themselves as creative geniuses who have the power to make people fall in love with products and forever influence public taste. They see themselves as slick and dashing and ahead of the proverbial curve standing on top of the world. Like Tom Wolfe's Sherman McCoy in *The Bonfire of the Vanities*, these people actually believe they are "Masters of the Universe."

What they don't realize is that the advertising they make often quite simply sucks. They're Don Draper alright…firmly planted in the retro world of advertising circa 1959, and quite frankly that's why the advertising they create is largely uninspiring and ineffective.

Stuck in the past

Over one half of all American households by 2011 will have DVR's that zap commercials with deadly efficiency. More than 19 million people listen to commercial-free satellite radio. Newspaper circulation is down six percent the last five years and dozens of heritage papers are on the verge of bankruptcy or closure. More than one billion people today have Internet access.

Despite these trends, most ad agencies continue to give clients much of the same advice they did in the 1950s. They advise them to purchase huge amounts of radio and television advertising and run full-page ads in newspapers and magazines.

The traditional ideas about advertising no longer work. The platforms on which messages are delivered have changed and the audience has gotten too sophisticated to fall for snake oil. As the Munchkin coroner said, "She's not only merely dead, she's really most sincerely dead." It's time to throw out everything about advertising that sucks – including inefficient delivery platforms like some television, radio, and print – and develop a new paradigm for harnessing customer awareness and developing sustained brand loyalty.

Business is not my business

There was a time when the ad man played a critical role in the growth of a business. The owner or CEO of the business (the client) – whether it was an oil company or a hot dog stand – was the expert at producing the product. If you were a widget maker[*], you were concerned with the cost of widgets, the availability of widget making materials, and how to best get them to customers. Your energies were focused on making quality widgets, maintaining a satisfied and qualified work force, and serving on the planning committee for next year's National Widget Association conference and golf outing in Puerto Vallarta.

What these widget makers – like other client product experts – didn't know how to do was market themselves to the trade. They had an accountant to handle their taxes and a lawyer to handle their legal disputes, but no one to advise how to publically position their product and generate new sales. Somewhere between setting up a booth at the World Widget Expo in Greenland and wondering why they're not featured in prominent trade books like *Widget Maker, What's a Widget Worth, the Widget News*, and *Harper's Bazaar*, they turned to advice

---

[*] Those were the days when we were still manufacturing damn good American-made widgets in this country, not importing our widget supply from the Far East or Latin America.

from an ad agency. Then the client could say, "I only know about making widgets. You guys make sure I'm in the right publications. You make sure I'm at the right business-to-business shows. You send out press releases about our newest Wiggle Widget®. Do everything you can to build an air war around our sales ground war."

It's very refreshing

Suppose you found yourself running a company that bottles Frosty Cola*. You'd hope your concoction of water, syrup, and fizz in a snazzy can would get into the hands of as many consumers as possible.

If Frosty Cola doesn't have some kind of *raison d'être*, some kind of unique position, why would anyone pick up a case of the stuff? There are too many other prominent soda brands on the supermarket shelves and convenience store coolers. You need to have some kind of unique value proposition for the product. You need to pay for slotting fees for a certain number of facings on supermarket shelves and all kinds of merchandising to bring the product closer to the consumer (while your advertising is working simultaneously to bring the consumer closer to your product).

Selling to a consumer is different than selling to a government procurement office or a widget-dependent manufacturer. You're not looking to make one sale; you're looking to make thousands. That's where the ad agency came in. Back in the Roaring '70s and '80s they would have taken all sorts of footage of girls in bikinis sipping Frosty Cola, while ultra-cool teenagers skate-boarded through a half-pipe in slow-motion. Then they would use your money to buy airtime and full-page ads in every media outlet in the country (taking a little piece of the action in the form of a tidy commission).

The ad man was necessary because neither the widget maker nor the soda bottler had the skills or the resources to do that kind of stuff themselves. To put it simply, advertising and marketing was not something they could handle in-house.

But now they can…

---

* Not a real soda. But if it were, it would come in diet, caffeine-free and assorted fruit flavors.

Step right up

It used to be an ad agency was the first place people went to create something, to come up with a Big Idea about a product. The ad men said, "We know how to do this. We can create a concept, come up with an ad, and run it all over the country." What they didn't tell the client until later was that they'd take about a 15% commission on all the media they placed for them. That was before all the rules changed.

We knew people were watching TV. They were a captive audience, sitting in their living rooms staring zombie-like at the blue light and grunting, "Errr…big box…me like*." We knew if we could get our client's product in front of that audience that we would very likely sell them some of it. What if the product didn't just advertise, but "sponsor" the program, actually produced the show? Now you're not just selling coffee, the product takes credit for your favorite show, the "Maxwell House Concert." And if we can put a bottle on the set, have the host smoke that brand, or be part of one of Jack Benny's gentle punch lines, all the better!

Soon advertising got increasingly worse. Not the groundbreaking stuff that David Ogilvy or Bill Bernbach made back in the day, which was based in data and fact with a strong creative execution. The next generation that came along had fallen in love with the "creative" and abandoned that portion of good advertising that dealt with the analytical. People were being creative for the sake of being creative. Or at least *trying* to be creative. Then TV ads moved away from the soft sell and back into the hard sell, and the commercials got even worse.

It continued that way for decades because 1.) It's all the ad agencies knew how to do, and 2.) The audience had nothing better to do.

The Flying Fickle Finger of Fate

Then things changed. People stopped watching television on television's terms. They began using VCR's to time-shift, to watch the shows they would otherwise miss and skip the commercials they would otherwise have to endure. Then came personal computers that made a funny noise when people would plug their modems into the telephone

---

* If reading this book aloud to others, please read this dialogue with your arms outstretched like Frankenstein's monster for maximum effect.

line. Their attention shifted from one light-up box to another. When the geeks increased the bandwidth, the computers got more like TVs, with audio and video from countless sources all at once stimulating our senses and entertaining us with rich "content." Then the TVs got more like computers, with digital-quality pictures, DVR functionality, and on-demand programming. The days were gone of Mom, Dad, 2.4 kids and Spot the Wonder Dog getting together in the living room to watch "Laugh-In."

The only problem was that the average ad agency didn't keep up with these changes. They were still like that Mad Man Don Draper, asking Goldie Hawn to "sock it to me." They were stuck in the same 1960s pattern of pumping out television commercials and buying up traditional media – in part because media commissions had become the crack cocaine of the advertising industry.

Agencies make very little margin on ad design and layout, even in producing TV commercials. They can make lots of money coordinating which stations or networks show the spots. They take a fee of up to 15% on the cost of that airtime (usually less than that today). Talk about a conflict of interest! The company asks its agency, "How much should we spend on advertising?" The agency, which gets a cut on every dollar their client spends, says, "Spend a lot! A whole lot!" Who's going to say, "Don't spend *too* much. You should put that cash into improving your packaging or rewarding great customer service"?

If one of the industry's gurus – Universal McCann's senior VP-director of forecasting Robert Coen – is correct, and advertisers spent a total of $42 billion on broadcast television (and another $16.3 billion on cable) in 2002, then ad agencies made $8.7 billion in media commission income just for acting as middle-men[*] between the broadcasters and the advertisers. What a country!

At half the price

There are many outside forces which now compete with the work once done exclusively by advertising agencies. Some of the fiercest

---

[*] I won't call them that other term for middle-men: "pimps." Pimps drive big cars, wear really bad fitting clothes, and try to get people to…wait…I guess we really could call them pimps.

competition for advertising clients and creative control of their advertising content came from the only other people who have all the equipment to make commercials: local radio and television stations. They argued to potential clients that advertising agencies were unnecessary for those who were just looking to be on TV or the radio. And they could do it at a fraction of the cost of those bloated agencies that only wanted the commissions and big creative fees anyway. The broadcast stations argued that their in-house production teams could cobble together something voiced by the morning DJ or shot with the same video cameras that the Action News crew used and get the client on the air fast and cheap.

And it was bad. Almost always bad. No professional ad agency dreamed up a TV commercial with a car dealer hitting a windshield with a sledge hammer to demonstrate how they're "smashing the competition!" Or told drive-time radio listeners to write down a telephone number while they were stuck in traffic. If you're looking for advertising that sucks, look no further than the crap produced by in-house production facilities of radio and TV stations. It was like they were trying to build a horse and instead got an ugly camel. The quality of the message didn't matter – the frequency did.

The placing of media is all too easy. Those radio and TV (or newspaper) salesmen would often say, "No need to use an agency to place this commercial on competing stations. I'll place those ads for you." Though some of the client's ad budget was going to the competition (as it would anyway), the individual salesperson could better influence what percentage of that budget was spent at their station or publication (no conflict there!).

The nearly-extinct agency

Today, unlike the early days of Madison Avenue, the average client's office has the tools in-house to produce its own advertising. If you have a computer on your desk, then you have the ability to design your own logos and letterhead (using one of a billion different fonts), to create professional looking leaflets and newsletters (using a desktop publishing program), or to mock up full-color ads to run in magazines or high school yearbooks (using photo editing and design templates). But you're also able to create web pages, blogs, upload business and sales-related photos and videos, and deploy direct mail or emails to existing or potential customers. With your PC, you become a creative director and a gatekeeper. There's virtually no New Media product (or Old Media product for that matter) that the average computer user can't make.

Just like the output of the local radio and TV stations, I won't vouch for the quality of anything made in-house by interns, receptionists, and accountants-come-ad designers. In fact, the quality of this homespun advertising may be even more dubious. The point is: *anyone can do this*. Any monkey* can buy media or design an ad. Do *you* need an ad agency to promote your business and move consumers to your product or service? Maybe, maybe not.

The 21st century ad agency

What does an ad agency look like in an age when fewer people are exposing themselves to advertising and everyone can be a gatekeeper? They can no longer create print ads and write broadcast copy alone. They can't simply design websites for clients.

A 21st century ad agency is not about the products it makes (commercials); it's about the services it provides (strategic planning and consulting) and then some.

1. They can no longer promote themselves as "advertisers."
Who wants to be an "advertiser"? Everyone knows advertising sucks. Nobody needs more advertising. What they need are marketing solutions. If your agency still says it does "advertising," you know they are on the verge of extinction.

Darren from "Bewitched" did *advertising*. But if Don Draper were around in the 2010s, he'd wear a custom tailored suit, greet you with a firm hand shake, and coolly say to you, "Oh, I'm in not advertising" (long pause while he stares at you with his steel-blue eyes, then takes a voluptuary drag on his Lucky Strike). And when you ask Draper what he does, he'd reply, "I'm a marketing innovator" (long sip from his very dry vodka martini†).

---

* No offense to monkeys.

† Three parts vodka, a sprinkle of dry vermouth, and a large olive served up with

2. They cannot call themselves an "agency."
Darren Stevens * worked at an agency: one of those bloated, insular institutions that bills for services just as mysterious as Endora's apparitions. Agencies belong to detectives, spies, insurance peddlers, and call girls. The term "agency" should be banished from the industry, lest people be reminded of advertising's wicked ways.

Calling it an "agency" is like calling a pharmacy an "apothecary." It's anachronistic. It's also voo-doo-istic. Call the business what it should be: a company or a firm – a marketing or creative resource.

3. They have to be media agnostic.
The business model has completely changed for today's marketers. Doing a media audit today (looking at reach and frequency data, determining cost per point) is like trying to catch a falling knife. It's constantly in flux, it's dropping so fast, and all that's going to happen to the advertiser is more likely than not to waste precious resources and get a disappointing result.

There will still be a need for making TV commercials; there will still be a desire to kill trees and print brochures. Today's marketing company will continue to do all the traditional functions of an old school ad agency. But they also need to be a strategic resource for their clients, providing advice for which media will best work at achieving their strategic marketing goals. If it means eschewing television in favor of the web, or dumping email to do radio, then do it if it makes good sense for the client, not good cents for the media buyer's compensation.

4. They have to provide services.
Market innovators are not just in the business of hawking products or services or institutions. They're also in the business of doing management consulting, reputation management, crisis

---

rocks on the side.

*   a.k.a. "Derwood."

communications, and cultivating an internal culture that can be exported to consumers with the deliberate goal of making the product "go viral."

Today's marketing innovation companies know that the purpose of any paid message is to direct potential consumers to a website (no longer getting them to "run, don't walk" or call the operators who are standing by) where they can experience the product and satisfy their appetite enough to get them to make that next step: purchase (either online or in a store). It's about increasing volume by getting a message exported directly to the customer on their time and their terms.

5. They have to provide content.
Ad men have always provided content in some form to their clients. Traditionally, it has been in the form of some craptastic commercial. Today, a marketing company should also offer editorial content to fill a company's website or blog. They should provide content for interactive social media, like Twitter or MySpace pages (as some widget makers are too busy making widgets to post daily updates on industry innovations themselves).

"Content" is different from "advertising." Marketing innovators are in the business of deploying relevant content to a relevant segment of the market through relevant mediums (could be traditional, could be web-based). That's how to enter into a dialogue with consumers, on their terms, giving them a reason to believe this product or service has the potential to have some positive effect on their lives.

6. They have to provide tools.
A marketing innovation company that doesn't suck also has to give its clients the tools to engage the consumer on a digital level. That means working with software developers and IT programmers to come up with web-based tools that will do just that (sometimes called, incidentally, "widgets").

Companies that are going to cultivate raving fans and harness their networks must have tools to do that, such as email platforms that allow senders to get data on who opened a message and who deleted it. Businesses with a web presence need templates to help them update their own content or deploy a podcast or streaming video. They need customer loyalty programs that capture data about the people using their products, learn what things they want more of, and market directly to them without the waste of traditional advertising.

7. They have to have something to show for it.
Today's marketing innovation company cannot simply buy a lot of air time and declare that their campaigns are successful. They need to use real metrics employed in web-based and interactive technology to catalogue who is listening and who isn't.

This is the one that scares the hell out of Darren Stevens, Mister Tate, and Uncle Arthur. Not because ad agencies cannot do it (although, getting that kind of empirical data from traditional media channels is nearly impossible), but because they don't want to do it. They don't want to pull the curtain back and show you how scattershot and ineffective their methods really are. They don't want clients to think they don't know what they're doing or that they're incompetent. Remember, these are the guys who believe they are "Masters of the Universe." They don't want you to know you could probably get the same results doing it yourself.

Get on the bandwagon

Some President once said something along the lines of, "If you're not with us, you're against us*." While the consequences aren't nearly that dire, that's sort of the place where advertising finds itself today. There is a fork in the road. Some advertisers will continue on the well-worn path; others will branch off and take a new way. Clients will follow them down one of the two roads.

Down one path are those who will continue to focus on old media principles, who will try to reach the largest amount of eyeballs regardless

---

* It might actually have been Anakin Skywalker in the final duel of "Revenge of the Sith."

of relevancy or waste. They'll go from one Darren (Dick Sergeant) to another Darren (Dick York), but still get the same results: advertising that sucks.

Down the other path are clients who have a dialogue with their consumers, who create networks of people who will evangelize for them. They are the ones who will create relevant content, not just more stupid commercials. They are the ones who will see their sales numbers increase. They are the ones who will use their ad dollars most effectively. They will succeed by increased awareness and market share.

And at the end of that path, like the Pied Piper of Hamelin, stands a cool sophisticated Don Draper, vodka martini in one hand, hot-looking moll on the other.

Chapter four

Dumb People Don't Make Things Any Easier

Internal culture exported

Advertising is not brain surgery, rocket science, or dynamite diffusion. It's not something that will get you or innocent bystanders killed. There *are* ads that bomb, but they don't endanger anything except brand perceptions and client relations.

That's not to say no one ever dies as a result of advertising. Consider those 1930s and 1940s advertisements claiming "20,679 physicians say [Lucky Strike cigarettes] are less irritating" or "More doctors smoke Camels than any other cigarette." All advertising is a form of propaganda and, in that sense, these messages are well-crafted. They implied that smoking was safe and healthy without having to provide any empirical evidence. From a pure messaging standpoint, these are good advertising campaigns. The problem is that these messages – which were duplicitous and perpetuated dangerous habits that contributed to the deaths of millions of Americans – were crafted by men and women who knew better. The "professionals" designed, shaped, and disseminated lies. The people who produced and marketed the tobacco were eventually hauled before Congress and given public reprimands for their culture of deceit, but the people who made the tobacco *advertising* were never really held accountable.

Part of the problem with advertising is the people *in* advertising. Anyone can claim to be an advertiser. There's no exam one must take. There's no degree one must obtain. There's no license one must hold. There's no training program one must complete. There's no government board of examiners one must answer to. There's no accreditation process. There's no real oversight, peer review, or accountability for any lack of verisimilitude. There's just the "free market" to sort out what is "good advertising" and who is able to create it.

Don't get me wrong. I'm not advocating for government intervention in marketing. What I *am* saying is there's a lot of wiggle room for ne'er-do-wells, scallywags, and nincompoops to go on dispensing advice on how to sell snake oil. Any monkey can do this. There are some very, very *incompetent* people who meet business owners and decision makers, look them in the eye, and tell them anything they want to hear about advertising. Their ideas are good because *they say* it's a good idea. That's how bad ads are born and millions of dollars are wasted. It's malpractice. A doctor or a lawyer who did that would get run out of town; ad men who have done it for years often get rich.

Falsehoods

"Ad men" – and I use the term derisively about the men *and women* who give my profession a bad name – often tell potential clients all sorts of things about the mystical powers of advertising, about what kind of witchcraft they can conjure to make people fall in love with them and spend lots of money. It's a great tale, isn't it? *You, Mister Product Manager, don't have to do anything other than make your product. I, the all-knowing, all-seeing advertising executive, will paint a portrait of you so alluring that people will dump buckets of money at your feet. The Great Oz has spoken!* It's a falsehood, of course. Consumers aren't the only ones advertisers lie to.

Here are some falsehoods that often get tossed around by the people trying to land your advertising business.

1. *Advertisers know how to make people want your product.* They like to make believe there is something about your world, your industry, and your product that only they know. If they don't impart this knowledge on you, you will not be a success. There is no Da Vinci's Code of marketing. The best way to kill a bad product is to advertise it well; the best way to kill a good product is to advertise it badly. There are

two elements to growing a business through marketing. First, you have to have a good product. Secondly, you have to promote it constantly in a manner that engages with and evolves with the consumer. The most successful campaigns come from a clear collaboration between the client (the person who knows the product best) and an advertising firm that can offer relevant counsel as to how best to market the product.

2. *If you advertise anything it will sell.* People are just too smart to fall for that one. They aren't going to buy a lot of crap[*]. At least, they're not going to buy a lot of crap *repeatedly*.

As a kid, do you remember seeing a toy on television that could do all sorts of amazing things, like jump over ramps or make machine gun noises? They never worked like that when you got them home, did they? They were smaller, less impressive, and frankly not nearly like what we saw on the tube. The centers of the cupcakes from the Easy-Bake Oven were always doughy[†] and the Evel Knievel motor bike trickster was never able to jump from the couch to the recliner, let alone across Snake River Canyon. It's the same thing with groceries and food products. A Big Mac never looks the way it does in the cardboard container as it does in the TV commercial. That's because the thing they're taking a picture of isn't actual food[‡].

All we want as consumers is what was promised to us. That seems fair, right? Consumers will always compare the product they have to the product that was promised through the advertising. So there has to be some reality to

---

[*]   Don't try to contradict me by pointing to the Snuggie. I have no rational explanation for that.

[†]   I never had an Easy-Bake Oven, but a girl I knew growing up had one. Let's just say at age 10 I was happy to judge her baking ability.

[‡]   There are food stylists who are using all sorts of paint thinner and Styrofoam to make a hamburger not wilt under the harsh lights of a studio. They pour white glue on bowls of breakfast cereal because milk appears blue on camera. It's a lie inside a fabrication wrapped up in bacon.

the claim. If the consumer says, "That's not the experience I had,'" they are going to be distrustful of both the product and the advertising. This will ultimately not help sales. Remember: advertising in and of itself cannot really sell anything. If done well, advertising can create a more effective selling environment in which people will try the products, hopefully become consumers, and then tell members of their respective book clubs[†].

3. *People will buy your product if a celebrity endorses it.* I'll get into this particular falsehood in detail in a later chapter, but in most cases celebrity endorsements just don't work. For one thing, celebrities are a dime a dozen these days. (See Paris Hilton, Balloon Boy, the Octo-mom, John and/or Kate) You can be famous for having ten babies, for sleeping with a politician, for being a loud-mouth blogger, or for sticking your kids in a runaway hot-air balloon. There are celebrities who are famous *for being famous.* It's like being a millionaire: it's not as big a deal as it used to be.

There are some cases in which the celebrity has some natural and inherent connection to a type of product which implies some amount of expertise (such as the glamorous movie star who sells eyeliner or the basketball player promoting a certain brand of shoe). These people aren't making the sale; they're getting the consumer's attention and making them think about certain characteristics of a product or service. No one thinks that Martina Hingis excelled at tennis because she wore Sergio Tacchini sneakers (nor do they believe her that "defective" Tacchini's were to blame for her athletic downfall).

Mostly, celebrities are used inappropriately for these endorsements. There's a difference between being a celebrity

---

[*] "When I bite into a York Peppermint Patty, I do *not* get the experience of crossing the frozen tundra." (Well, we'll let this one slide as a byproduct of metaphoric creative license.)

[†] In my wife's eyes, the ultimate validation to one's network which surely means more sales.

endorser and being a paid spokesman. Muhammad Ali was the greatest heavyweight fighter of all time and he sold d-Con pest strips on television in the 1980s. (d-Con didn't *beat up* cockroaches; it just poisoned them. Apparently Claus von Bülow was unavailable.)

4. *If you don't advertise, you'll never be a success.* It may be an unconventional tack, and it won't pay my mortgage, but you really don't have to advertise in order to attract customers. It's a law of business nature that good products, services, and establishments will find their way to customers (and vice-versa). Good products sell; bad ones don't – at least not for long.

For almost 75 years, the Hershey Chocolate Corporation never conducted a national advertising campaign. Still, for many Americans, the taste of a Hershey's bar or Kiss is what milk chocolate is supposed to taste like. Started in 1894, Hershey's was a recognized brand in shops and markets across the country. During World War II, more than 24 million "Field Ration D" Hershey bars a week were given to servicemen as part of their daily diet. The popularity of the candy only increased with GI's and Baby Boomers in peacetime. It wasn't until 1970 that the great American chocolate bar appeared in its first TV commercial.

When the Ad Man says you can't succeed without advertising, he means advertising through traditional media. But these days consumers are most likely to find you through a Google search conducted when they're about to make a purchase. For some businesses, a good website can be enough.

One cannot underestimate the power of a viral referral. Hershey's thrived for decades on what essentially was "word of mouth" advertising: homemaker to homemaker, school kid to school kid. Today, we're connected to *all* of our friends and acquaintances in digital networks. If one person tweets about your sandwich shop's meatball special or your car dealership's stellar service department, they've praised you in front of the 100, 200, or 500 people in their networks in one shot.

Internal culture exported

Advertising in the new digital age is all about exporting your product, company, or institution's internal culture. Businesses must get their customers to understand and buy into their philosophies, style, and mantra. They must move their mission statement from inside the boardroom to the other side of the cash register. When customers buy into your culture – not just buy your product – they will become repeat customers. Repeat customers become fans who then become evangelists for you and your products. You sell more products, introduce brand extensions, become an iconic brand, and ultimately sell out to a giant multi-national company (probably from Asia) for a ton of money and move to an upscale minimum-security gated community on a golf course in South Florida.

If I removed all the signage inside the store, could you tell whether you were in a Walmart or a K-Mart? If you've been to Walmart, you've noticed the blue smocks, the greeters, the ample aisle space, and the emphasis on low prices. K-Mart – now owned and operated by Sears – doesn't have the same distinctive culture on display (or the same successful grip as the number one retailer in the free world).

There are many businesses that export cultures that distinguish and differentiate themselves from their competitors. From a cultural point of view, is Frederick's of Hollywood different than Victoria's Secret? Is The Sharper Image different from Brookstone? Is TGIFriday's different from Texas Roadhouse? Is the Pottery Barn different from Restoration Hardware? Is Ben & Jerry's different from Häagen-Dazs?

Each one of these retailers or products has a style or position that is their own. The position may not be superior or unique (Häagen-Dazs also sells premium ice cream, but only Ben & Jerry's*is associated with socially-conscious business practices); however, they are clearly identifiable. It's the emotional connections that consumers make with these corporate cultures that make them fans and marry them to products as long term customers. (Oh, and by the way, these are all good products to boot!)

---

* Frankly, I personally believe the only reason the Rain Forest still exists is because these two socialists from Vermont started selling pints of ice cream.

Doctor, doctor, give me the news

Over the years, I've worked with many hospitals on image and service line campaigns. Examining it from a very high level, one can say all hospitals are the same. We all know that, with the exception of certain specialty or tertiary services, specific technologies, or procedures unique to individual providers, one hospital isn't radically different from another (especially those rare community hospitals not already owned by someone else). Medicine is medicine; we don't have a *McDonald's* hospital and a *Red Lobster* hospital. People who are sick go to hospitals for treatment (usually the closest one, especially if an ambulance is involved). Their expectations are to get well.

How do certain hospitals grow to become thought of as leaders in their primary and secondary service areas? How do some achieve the most desirable clinical reputations, increase awareness, preference, and market share? How do others get tagged with bad reputations?

One of the most innovative health care executives I've worked with is Alyson Pitman Giles, the CEO of Catholic Medical Center in Manchester, NH. She understands that effective, targeted marketing can help improve awareness for a provider. Highlighting clinical service lines and raising awareness among patients through mass media can help. But Alyson also fundamentally gets it that it's not the advertising or the new da Vinci robotic surgical suite that makes a perceptual difference about the provider in patients' minds. It's the nurses who shape the patients' experience with the institution!

Happy patients and their families will spread the word, making a health care provider's services and reputation "go viral." For all of Alyson's aggressive strategic planning, physician relations, and the ongoing effort to build an internal culture within her organization, she has also never lost sight of the importance of engaging key stakeholders to get their help spreading the message. Alyson's sense of market research, the changing health care landscape, and her ability as a natural motivator are all important assets. But it's her "gut" I really admire. Like so many effective marketing-centric executives she just naturally creates a culture of communication that is exported to every potential fan of the institution.

We've found that among the factors that influence customer/patient satisfaction and the reputation of a health care provider is the personal relationship and interaction with their nurse. That's the employee they have the most contact with, the one who is most likely going to shape their experience with and perception of the institution's quality of care. Talk to any mother of a newborn and they're likely to rave about how the maternity nurses comforted them and helped them. The Emergency Room staff might have expertly set the broken arm, but it was the way they responded and reassured the patient after the car accident that fostered the confidence toward recovery.

When a loved one passes away, it is the sympathy and respectful dedication from the medical staff that affirmed for relatives that the care administered was the best possible.[*]

In these examples, the nurses *exported the internal culture* of the hospital to the patients. They portrayed an aura of professionalism, compassion, and excellence. The patients felt it and left the hospital as advocates for that brand of care[†]. Even if the medical results were less than optimal (i.e. *death*), they still were highly satisfied with the care because of the relationship they had with the nurses (or physicians or therapists or other clinical professional). But the nurses are on the front line of delivering the service, so I give them the credit.

Access to good care is another thing. Your kid breaks his arm so you take him to the local emergency room. They do a great job – but you wait 4 ½ hours before the doctor even sees you. Ultimately, you got what you came for – and hopefully Little Johnny still has a shot at pitching for the Sox one day – but you will certainly let the people in your network know that it took too long and the experience was "unpleasant."

In health care, it's the nurses. In other industries, it's the people in the trenches who make a difference. The people who man the phones,

---

[*] Can you imagine being in any other line of work in which one of your paying customers *dies* and their relatives walk away grateful for your services. I've had clients throw coffee mugs at me because they didn't like my ad copy. I can't *fathom* what they'd do to me if someone dropped dead in the middle of a commercial shoot.

[†] Speaking of "brands of care," hospitals are literally branding certain medical techniques or procedures and licensing them to other facilities. What better way can you get Boston-quality cancer care or Hollywood-style plastic surgery in your small-town hospital than to go to a "Mayo Clinic" clinic or the "Cedars-Sinai" affiliated hospital?

who work the register, who deliver the food – they are as much a part of a business's success as the brainiacs in the board room.

We love to fly and it shows

Another example of exported culture is occurring in the airline industry. There once was a time when there was something very exotic – even glamorous – about traveling by air. People got "dressed up" to fly and would dine (in the truest sense of the word) at the airport restaurant before making their way to the departure lounge. Even the stewardesses (that was their name – I'm not going to re-write history and call them "flight attendants" just to be politically correct) wore snazzy designer-inspired uniforms. Getting a mid-flight cocktail was *de rigueur*. Everyone onboard was en route to some kind of adventure, be it vacation or business. Each traveler was an explorer.

Today, flying is, simply put, a hassle. Security measures in a post-9/11 world have made it impossible to park at the curb, pack liquids in a carry-on, or wear our shoes through a metal detector. The fact that the terrorists have now invented exploding underwear will certainly not make your experience at airport security any more expeditious either. The flights are no better. There's no leg room. There's no movie. It's hot and cramped. You're lucky if the amenities include a second bag of peanuts and a very small can of soda. What's worse is a flight anywhere in your own time zone will still probably run about $400 on a good day. Those are not very friendly skies.

If you've ever flown on Southwest Airlines, however, you know they try to provide an experience that's, well…different. Their success is not just in the fact that their price point is competitive or that their airplane turn-around times are fast. The company's founders, Rollin King and Herb Kelleher, made it part of the mission to actually make no-frills fun.

Southwest's flight attendants[*] do more than offer coffee, tea, or milk. They wear khakis and polo shirts instead of those quasi-military flight uniforms. They tell jokes during the pre-flight instructions ("There may be 50 ways to leave your lover, but there are only 4 ways out of this aircraft…"). They do the Southwest Hokey Pokey. They sing Happy

---

[*] In this case, I'll stipulate to the fact that's their title.

Birthday. They play up the fact that they are no-frills, embracing the idea that you'll get one – count 'em – one bag of peanuts. Most importantly, the planes are clean, the people are nice, and at least as I write this there is no additional charge to bring a suitcase with you when you travel.

Just like those nurses, Southwest's customer service staff does a great job exporting their corporate culture to travelers. People who fly on Southwest *get it*. They understand that Southwest is giving a wink and a nod to the shortcomings of their industry. Now they're the Gold Standard for what a profitable low-cost carrier ought to be. If the other airlines are like the matronly school marms, Southwest is like the cool gym teacher who has no problem with gum chewing or singing during homeroom. They "luv" to fly and frankly it really does show!

Are we there yet?

Now, consider for one moment if the flight attendant spills your complementary beverage in your lap or one of those nurses tells you to stop complaining about your obstructed duodenum. Your perception of the service you received will be tainted. Even if everything else about the product or service was exceptional, even if the deficiencies were not the organization's fault, you're less likely to provide further business or recommend them to others.

A company or its product will never satisfy one-hundred percent of their customers one-hundred percent of the time. But no one can afford to have one percent of their customers feel like they didn't listen to them and at least try to make it better.

If someone dining at a restaurant complains to the manager about the entrée, the manager needs to listen. Maybe he can satisfy the guest's concerns, offer a spiff that is equal in value to the perceived deficiency. Regardless, the customer has to feel like they got a fair shake. There was a time when someone could puff themselves up and make the hollow threat that, "I'm going to tell everyone I know never to come here again." That never worked; most folks don't have that kind of time or juice. Today, people of any caste or station can say, "I'm going to post on my blog/my webpage/my Twitter account and tell everyone never to come here." Now the threat is no longer contained to the few people to whom this diner might actually recount the transgression. They *can* actually tell everyone they know with a few keystrokes – as well as the friends of their friends. The service complaint can go viral. Good news travels fast. Bad news travels faster.

A musician named Dave Carroll got the runaround from United Airlines after his $3,500 Taylor guitar was broken on his Halifax-to-Chicago-to-Nebraska flight. In July 2009, after a year of being unable to get the airline to pay for the damages, Carroll created a music video called "United Breaks Guitars." In it he lampooned the buffoonish baggage handlers, the indifferent flight attendants, and singled out a "Ms. Irlweg" who refused his claim. The video was watched 6.6 million times on YouTube and became all the rage as it was then re-reported in the mainstream media. United, belatedly, offered to pay Carroll for the instrument, an offer the musician promptly rejected. It seems revenge is a dish best served with musical accompaniment.

Ask JetBlue, another discount carrier, what the pitfalls are of not paying attention to that one percent of their customers. During one winter storm in February 2007, dozens of flights out of New York were grounded. On Flight 751 bound for Mexico, passengers were kept on the runway for eight long hours. Citing FAA regulations, the flight attendants refused to hand out food and water (even to two diabetic passengers). The plane had no power and the crew had to keep open the ice-covered doors to let fresh air into the plane. Disgruntled travelers began to text and cell phone their families and news organizations about being "held hostage" by JetBlue on the tarmac. One passenger spoke live on CNN from her cell about the deplorable conditions on board while the anchor broadcasted footage of JetBlue's fleet stuck in the blizzard. There was a near mutiny, as the crew refused the passengers' demands that they return to the gate and allow them to de-plane.

What made this event so damaging to JetBlue was it had already built its marketing campaign – its internal culture – on customer service. The problem might have been contained had the crew of Flight 751 done a better job of exporting that internal culture that day they were stranded on the tarmac. Prior to the storm, JetBlue had among the highest customer service rankings from *BusinessWeek*. During that one week, JetBlue cancelled 1,100 flights affecting 130,000 travelers[*].

---

[*] The service meltdown wasn't just due to snow. After the weather broke, aircraft and staff were scattered across the country out of position. A computer snafu made

The public relations debacle cost JetBlue $30 million dollars and its stock dropped five percent. A contrite CEO David Neeleman went on *The Late Show* with David Letterman to apologize and offer a service guarantee – the Passenger's Bill of Rights – which promised vouchers in certain situations for future delays. But it doesn't matter how many free tickets you give out. You're only as good as your brand perception was a second ago.

Pulling it together

In order to be successful in a world where more people are likely to read the tweet than actually see the apology on TV, brands and institutions have to develop and refine their corporate culture and discover ways to bring what is best about them to the customer on a consistent basis. They can't afford to have drones working at the cash register or answering tech service calls. Everyone in the organization must buy into the idea of *who they are*, of what their internal culture is all about. And they must start taking advantage of social media channels to push that culture. Otherwise some competitor will.

They should also try to keep the number of dumb ad and PR guys to a bare minimum and surround themselves with marketers who understand what the digital future means for their consumer channel. If your ad agency still wants to market your business like it's 1974, tell them to get an advertising license – just so somebody can revoke it.

---

rescheduling difficult. It was described by industry observers as one of the worst non-crash-related weeks for any airline.

Chapter five

I Always Wanted the Job Spielberg Has

The necessity of creativity

Every person who directs a TV commercial (as I have) dreams about directing a major motion picture. It's easy to do (dream about the movies, that is). You start with casting. You do wardrobe. (Well in my case, I don't do it, but some wardrobe fashionista does it and then makes it easy by saying, "What do you think about the tie? Red or blue?") You demand re-writes. On set, there are huge lights and expensive sound equipment with fuzzy microphones that look like dead raccoons on a stick. There's a crew of anywhere from five to fifty people, most of them picking their noses while you decide how to make the milk in the cereal look more like milk[*]. If you're on location, they build a track so the strongest dude on the crew can smoothly push the camera dolly back and forth during a shot. You get to sit in a big chair and bark commands about your "vision." They even have gophers who make union wages to take your lunch order and ask if you'd like a spring water. Not to mention the craft services table which provides snacks all day and night to give energy, inspiration, and higher cholesterol levels to everyone involved.[†]

Just like James Cameron or Steven Spielberg, I take pride in the commercials I make and I think of them as little pieces of art. I try hard

---

[*] Remember: the answer is to use white glue.

[†] This is called "craft services," and is a way to bill the client for the coffee and sandwiches the crew eats between takes. That's why it's not called "catering."

not to make advertising that sucks. It may be 30 seconds of hawking a product to you, but I view it as a mini-movie.

For all my ranting about the short-shrift that research and empirical data gets, I'm really drawn to the creative side of the advertising business. There is a necessity for creativity in advertising, but it's sometimes hard to find. I enjoy rough cuts of commercials, colorful story boards, brilliant set design, and cleverly-written copy. And at this point in my career I feel that over the years our team has done some kick ass campaigns.

And it's all because I hate math.

In the beginning

I attribute my successful career in advertising, marketing, and public relations to Sister Theresa St. Pierre at Trinity High School in Manchester, NH. I had her for Algebra I in my freshman year. Sister Theresa was a very small, very tough nun – the kind the Vatican was secretly stockpiling in case they ran another Inquisition. She was not a terribly nurturing human being, but she knew her algebra.

I was always the class clown, cracking jokes and trying my best to make the experience more bearable for the rest of the class. I never had any trouble with a teacher. I did my homework, passed it in. Even if I didn't totally grasp what they were teaching, I completed the work and usually charmed my way toward a gentleman's B.

However, at some point in my life as a student I developed a "math-phobia." Sister Theresa would give the class algebra problems to work on while I used the time to doodle cartoons in the margins of my notebook. I regularly enjoyed cartooning as a kid and was pretty good at it. My caricatures of teachers were a big hit with my classmates; however, the caricature I drew of Sister Theresa one particular day – that she discovered me creating in mid-pencil stroke – did little to improve the tenor of our relationship*. When it came time to work out algebra problems on the board, she almost *always* called on me. She did it because she knew I didn't get it (which was obvious by the flurry of letters and numbers I was randomly placing around the equation). "No,

---

* Ironically, this is a bit of bad luck that also befell my collaborator, Kevin Flynn, while he was at Holyoke Catholic High School. Latin teacher Sister Agnes Loretto discovered his unflattering rendering of her during first declensions.

that's wrong Patrick. Sit down." And I would dejectedly stride back to my seat.

My friends wanted to be doctors or engineers, lawyers or financiers. But those were all things that involved (gulp) math. I needed to do something else that didn't involve square roots, Pythagorean theorems, or a slide rule. I needed something more creative.

Getting a foot in

I decided to use my powers for good instead of evil. All those cartoons I had done of teachers and classmates convinced me that I could make money doing caricatures. I made it my summer job. In the mid '70s I'd drive my Plymouth Duster all over New England and set up at a shopping mall or a county fair and do caricatures for ten bucks a whack. I made a lot of money doing that*. It became a show as people gathered around to debate whether the drawing matched the subject, whether it looked good or not. Through the interactions with the crowd, I learned how to entertain and to sell. I found that the more entertained the people were, the more likely they were to get in line for a caricature themselves. *Cha-ching!* It was a good living and actually wound up helping me pay for college!

In 1976, while still in high school, I visited the office of a hotshot young advertising guy who was new in town. Gary O'Neil started an agency called O'Neil Jalbert and Gould; he was young and brash and did great work. I asked if he'd take a look at my portfolio and give me some advice. "You're really good, kid," he said. "Come back when you have a little more experience." I liked Gary from the moment I met him and at the time had little idea that our paths would cross again.

There were other people who were advocates and inspirations for me. My parents were incredibly supportive (it was actually their Plymouth Duster). My neighbor, Bob Montgomery, a well-respected player at the former Weston Advertising Agency and professor at Boston University School of Public Communications, was extremely encouraging taking an early interest in my graphic art talent and teaching me about the ad business. The late Al Sprague, the founder of the Bedford Granite Group and president of the New Hampshire Association of Broadcasters, was

---

* In fact on a good day I could do about 50 caricatures. Do the math!

also someone who was both friend and competitor for many years. Al once told me "Don't sell 'em what you want, sell 'em what they want." In other words, give the *client* what they want. No sense slowing commerce. Al was a hell of a good guy whose longevity in the business was a true rarity. All these people were generous with their time and opinions and provided much appreciated direction and inspiration in the early part of my career.

Shucking Oysters

In the 1980s as a student at Stonehill College in North Easton, Massachusetts, I began to study marketing communications and psychology with the thought that I would become an art director or graphic designer. The psychology part was there because if marketing didn't work at least I would have the option of messing with people's minds (Yes, I was slightly cynical – even as an undergraduate). I got the best job any college student could get: I was an on-campus representative for Anheuser-Busch.[*] I was issued framed mirrors, neon signs, and T-shirts that said "Budweiser" on them – which increased my popularity with my friends and a number of the ladies on campus. I also had a "trade spending account" so I could purchase Bud products for people going to a bar or planning keg parties. What I learned from the experience is 1) A sales person with a good product or brand can do well influencing his market place, and 2) Cheerleaders would do almost anything to get a free t-shirt[†].

Another activity I got involved with was running the school's marketing club. My responsibility was to line up speakers to come to campus and share their perspectives. Of course, my real motivation for attempting to contact all these captains of industry was that I wanted to get a job when I graduated. So I invited them to speak, which usually involved me taking them to dinner before the gig when I would

---

[*] The drinking age in Massachusetts at the time was 18. College students didn't need a lot of encouragement to purchase beer. Even *I* couldn't screw this up – even if there was a little math involved in the form of a monthly sales report.

[†] The great irony is that today I am a member of the Stonehill College Board of Trustees and I have sat through many a Dean's speech about community standards and the challenges of student compliance with the alcohol policy in this day of the legal drinking age being 21. I feel like a bit of a pariah!

promptly hustle them for internships and jobs and slip them a copy of my résumé.

Most of the speakers were very good and eager to share their experiences with the students. There was one little company in nearby Randolph, MA that I kept pestering, trying in vain to get the Senior VP of Product Marketing to call me back. Every few days I would call this then family-run business, Dunkin Donuts of America, and get pushed through to the man's assistant. The guy had a great name: Duffy Oyster. Each time I'd leave a message for Mr. Oyster to call me but he never did. Finally, in an act of desperation, I said to the secretary, "Just tell Duffy that it's his old friend, Pat, and see if he can get back to me." I left her the number of the phone outside my dorm room. Not long after that the phone rang and it was Mr. Oyster himself.

"Who is this?" he said, searching his memory bank for an old friend named Pat. I came clean, told him I was a Stonehill College student, and asked if he would be interested in speaking at the college. Duffy laughed his ass off and rewarded my ingenuity by agreeing to come to the school and give a talk. We set a date. The deal was done.

Duffy's speech covered Dunkin Donuts' plans to expand its brand, to move away from being a doughnut-and-coffee place and become the modern neighborhood bakery. They wanted to bake muffins and cookies. They wanted to do funny things with the wasted dough they disposed of daily*. They wanted to expand beyond New England and become a national brand.

After his speech I followed him back to his car, working up the courage to ask if he in fact had an internship available. Duffy, still chuckling about the phone message I left, thought I was one of the gutsiest hucksters he had ever run into and told me to come on down to his office for an interview. He knew that I had decided that Dunkin Donuts on my resume represented, at least in my mind, the chance to perhaps make some real "dough" in the future.

---

*   Doughnut dough gets extremely tough after it's been used, so the scrap pieces won't bond like cookie dough. DD's created the "Dunkin Munchkin" quite literally out of the doughnut holes left behind in an effort to recycle its resources and reduce costs. The rest is history and profit.

Time to make the doughnuts

Being at Dunkin Donuts during the early 1980s at a time of real planned growth was fascinating. Working in product marketing, I'd be given sales and marketing reports to analyze. I'd often get the Sister Theresa-terror-sweats when I had to jigger all the numbers, but it was fairly basic math which I could handle[*]. They put me in charge of a project to study whether DDs could create a really good "fresh-brewed" iced-tea product. I was calling tea-growers all over the world, taste-testing in the company's corporate kitchen, gathering data and hosting numerous potential tea purveyors in Randolph. The funny thing was none of the people knew I was an intern and most treated me like a VP.

I also got to sit in on Duffy's meetings with the New York and Boston ad agencies that Dunkins engaged. These guys would fly in to show their creative concepts for product roll outs we were working on. At the time, DD's was about to launch the first Dunkin Munchkins campaign and was exploring whether to offer a Dunkin Donuts brand of premium ice cream in their stores as well. These agency guys (usually dressed in trendy black garb) would show us comps of point of sale pieces and other in-store merchandising as well as scripts and storyboards for TV commercials. I – the college intern – had the audacity to bring occasionally to the meetings my own layouts of what the tent cards and store window posters might look like. I wrote headlines and body copy. I freely shared my ideas, scribbled on a legal pad, to Duffy and the marketing staff and the clearly-miffed agency guys.

"This is really good!" Duffy said one day. That pissed off the New York guys to no end that some college gopher was showing them up in front of their client. That's when I knew I could do it, that I could be successful in advertising. I knew my copy and layouts were good; all I really needed were the black duds.

This Bud's for you

After graduation, I took a job with Anheuser-Busch St. Louis, working around the region and the country on field marketing strategy

---

[*] With the help of a trusty calculator.

for the King of Beers. I traveled a lot and missed my friends and family in New England, skiing in the White Mountains, and the bars of my beloved Boston. So I decided against a career with the brewer and took a job with an A-B distributor in Manchester, NH, Great State Beverages, run by a long time family friend, Bob Koslowsky. Based on my knowledge of advertising and my experience with the brewery, they made me Director of Sales and Marketing.

Around that time, Anheuser-Busch was increasing its portfolio of product offerings by launching Michelob Light and wanted its distributors to really push the product. A-B was *par excellence* at motivating its sales force to sell, sending guys on vacations or trips to the Super Bowl. And by "guys," I literally mean "men," because at the time there were very few women in the beer business. Nothing underscored exactly how much of a man's world it was in the early '80s than when St. Louis launched a Michelob Light sales promotion in 1983.

I'll never forget unrolling the poster they sent and seeing 12 gorgeous women seated at a bar toasting with Mich Light bottles and mugs. The slogan for the promotion was "Win Yourself a Playboy Playmate!" The idea was simple: increase your Michelob Light sales by a certain percentage over the previous sales quarter and the Playboy Playmate of your choice would visit your market to help "promote" the brand. All the guys in the office ogled the poster, sizing up each of the girls like a butcher might size up a proverbial fatted calf. The boss, Bob , walked into the room, pointed right to Miss February 1980 (35 ½ -25-35 ½), and said he liked that one. As they say, he was the boss, so the issue of which of these lovely woman would come to our market was settled. Now all we had to do was win the promotion.

I went to work along with the sales manager pushing for more case sales, draught placements, and point of sale materials in the stores, as well as increased radio advertising and sales incentives.

Sure enough, we won the contest and won the privilege of a market visit from Miss February, Sandy Cagle*. Not only did we win, but another New Hampshire distributor also won a visit from *another*

---

* Turn-ons: Men with brown eyes, a crisp fall morning, Old English sheep dogs, suntans, roller skating. Turn-offs: Jealousy, riding on the bus, rude people, crowded elevators, cigar smoke. [True facts] playmate. These two young ladies traveled together (unaccompanied) to Boston's Logan Airport to discover twelve over-served beer salesmen in a tricked-out Anheuser-Busch mobile home waiting to escort them back to New Hampshire. They were brave and beautiful. They also turned out to be great at PR and promotion – all things they undoubtedly gleaned from "Hef" during their time at the mansion.

I scheduled all kinds of press interviews and personal appearances for Sandy; I was all business about this opportunity. But Bob had other ideas. When the promotional tour was over, he decided to keep her – literally! He had left his wife after a messy divorce and fell in love with Sandy. We were all stunned, jealous, and more than a little impressed. One worker, worried about raising the ire of Anheuser-Busch executives in St. Louis, wondered aloud, "I think the rules are we have to give her back." Mr. Koslowsky decided against it (They were married a couple of years later and remain happily together to this day).

Three's company

Bob Koslowsky was always very good to me. He understood that I wanted to be in advertising and that I would probably soon leave his company to find ad work in Boston. His new bride, Sandy, was not only sweet and beautiful, but she was extremely savvy. Working through Playboy Enterprises with different sponsors, Sandy had an excellent understanding of how the PR business went. We decided to form our own agency, Eagle Advertising, emblematic of the Anheuser-Busch eagle that brought us all together. I would do creative and account work; Sandy would do some sales; Bob was the money man, and A-B and a number of its distributors helped form the early members of our fledgling client roster.

We were able to hire a secretary, an art director, and pay a couple of consultants, including the aforementioned Bob Montgomery who proved to be invaluable. Our office in the Bedford building looked like a 1940s detective agency (I was always waiting for some dame to show up and say her husband was missing or cheating). Bob and some of the other New Hampshire A-B distributors were among our first clients, as well as Anheuser-Busch itself and its Eagle Snacks brand. We were able to earn some instant credibility in the region even though we were very much unproven. And Sandy was our secret weapon, because everyone she met wanted to take a meeting with her*. Eagle Advertising was soon a hot property in the agency space. We began to sign more clients and staff and we began to win business against some of our more established and experienced competitors.

Everywhere we were going, looking for new business, we kept running into the aforementioned Gary O'Neil, the guy who once gave me career guidance in high school. The Manchester ad man of O'Neil Jalbert and Gould was now doing business as O'Neil & Associates (Jalbert and Gould had gone off to do their own things by that time). Sometimes our agency would get the business, sometimes his would get it. There was resentment among some players in the industry. Here was this kid and a Playboy playmate spending someone else's money challenging the old guard agencies in New Hampshire and beyond. I was 22 at the time!

Eagle Advertising continued to grow. Bob and Sandy traveled often, leaving me to mind the shop. I wanted to own the business, but discussions with Bob about selling to me weren't very productive. I was becoming frustrated and slightly restless. Then one dark winter afternoon, the phone ran. It was Gary O'Neil. "Let's have a drink," he said. We met at some obscure restaurant (I think it was a Pizza Hut) and started talking business. "It's crazy for you and me to be competing against each other," O'Neil said. "We should team up, work together. Let's see what we can do to bring the companies together."

Everyone that I trusted told me it would never work. They said you can't have two roosters in the barnyard† and Gary O'Neil had a track record of going through partners like most people change their underwear. Like Ernest Borgnine and Ethel Merman or J-Lo and Ben Affleck, no one gave us a chance.

When the newly formed O'Neil Griffin and Associates opened, we had seven employees. Gary and I shared an office because we needed room (and the furniture came with the lease). Within five years, we had 60 employees. I had become a full-partner in the firm and my

---

* If Sandy had a lunch meeting, I would often go along and sit between her and a male client to make sure the guy really had some business to offer. More hands wound up on my thigh than on Sandy's. (I felt so cheap!)

† They all said it was hard to tell which one of us was the bigger rooster.

relationship with Gary lasted 15 years[*]. Gary remains one of those iconic advertising legends whose creativity, wit, and pure ballsy attitude helped change the agency business in New England. In 2004, I bought him out and today, I am CEO and Chairman of the company which Gary originally formed, and has been successfully kicking around, in one form or another, since 1975. Today, Griffin York & Krause (GY&K) celebrates three decades in business and still has some key employees who have been there since before me! Elaine Krause, Rose Longo-White, Gloria Proulx, Grace Sheehan, you know who you are! Those women are amazingly talented and loyal and without them GY&K would not be the success it is today.

My bona fides

In my many years of advertising, I've watched the industry move from client-focused ads to product-focused ads, move from broadcast media to online media. I've worked with major national corporations and tiny non-profits. I've worked with dozens of political candidates, from statewide races to the presidential candidates and Presidents themselves who crisscross New Hampshire every four years for our first in the nation Presidential primary.

I'm not just the old crank shaking his fist at the sky. When I say "advertising sucks," I'm not throwing bombs. I have the years of experience – and quite humbly, the talent – and an amazing team of collaborators to recognize what does and does not work.

I also think I have a good handle on how our business is in a constant state of evolution. The lessons I have learned are applicable to all kinds of clients and business products. It's not a cookie cutter approach by any means – some industries or products are better suited for social media and the interactive strategies we espouse (Let's face it: people are more likely to become online fans of something fun, like the lottery or a resort, than an industrial provider or an equipment manufacturer who markets its wares in a B2B manner).

Steven Spielberg and James Cameron have a knack for making movies with romanticized characters, dramatic scores, and sweeping storylines. Whether it's "E.T." or "Titanic" or "Schindler's List," people

---

[*]   Longer than any of Liz Taylor's marriages

have great affection and respect for the work. They fall in love with it. So I guess in that way, I *am* just a tiny bit like Spielberg and Cameron. I too have been trying to make people fall in love. Instead of globe-trotting archeologists and sinking ocean liners, I've spent my career trying to get them to fall in love with doughnuts, barbeque sauce, beer, or their local hospital.

And in spite of the fact that media analysis, cost per clicks, quantitative research, and the micro-segmentation of data are a big part of what we do…let's just say I'm fortunate to have really smart people around me who do that stuff a lot better than I do. So for me, at least, there's thankfully not much math.

Sister Teresa – wherever you are – thanks for steering me away from nuclear fission and into this amazing, creative, and rewarding business called "advertising."

Chapter six

P.T. Barnum Had it Right

(At least for a while)

It was called "The Greatest Show on Earth." No one who ever saw the original P.T. Barnum's circus is still around, but we'll take old Phineas Taylor's word on it. Why not? No one else had the audacity to claim such a title[*].

Even though he had great faith in his performers, Barnum knew that not everybody would like every act. That's why he and his partner, William Cameron Coup, invented the three-ring circus. Barnum knew that if you didn't like the sword swallower in one ring, you might like the acrobats in another. If you didn't like the clowns, you might like the fire-eater or Jumbo the elephant.

Barnum had stumbled upon a very important concept in getting and holding his audience's attention, one that's even truer today. He developed one of the first models of market segmentation. He did not look at his audience as one large mass, agreeable to all the spectacle and humbug he could parade in front of them. He knew his audience had different tastes and certain acts would be favored by some – and some by others.

Instead of alienating part of his audience with content that didn't appeal to them, Barnum segmented his content so he could please every part of it. The Greatest Show on Earth was not about one big act

---

[*] There *was* this show I saw in Tijuana that involved a masked woman, three chickens, and a donkey. If we really had to start ranking shows, I'd probably vote it as the second greatest. That, however, is another story.

that everyone would love; it was about creating enough acts that every fraction of the audience could be satisfied.

In order to make really effective marketing today, you have to have a little of P.T. Barnum in you.

The first cut isn't the deepest

Market segmentation is about finding your customer, being helpful so they can get to you, continuing to give them what they want, and not trying to be something other than what you generally are.

We used to talk about market segmentation in ways such as this: we could subdivide our audience into some broad demographic or psychographic profile. We could split them up by gender, by zip code, by education level, by whether or not they were a sports fan. It was pretty much the view from 30,000 feet. *What's your name? What's your salary? What's your religion? How many times a month do you buy toilet paper?* It was usually enough to complete a survey or fit individuals into some segment of the population. We considered it extremely helpful at the time, allowing us to cross tabulate data and find trends. Today, this same data tells us almost nothing.

Market segmentation sucks. *Micro*-market segmentation is where it's at. That's the segmentation of market segmentation. It's subdividing those subdivisions of people into smaller, more precise, even obscure groups of people. If we need to find little old ladies who live east of the river, drive blue cars, and have had cataract surgery as well as a penchant for mini schnauzers, we can target them.

I found my thrill

For the sake of this story, let's assume you're single and you're looking for a date for this weekend.* Instead of getting a date the way you used to do it – church socials, ads in the newspaper, consuming large amounts of Jägermeister and waiting for bar flies to take advantage of your suggestive state of mind – you're going to micro-segment your network.

---

* Technically, you don't need to be single to be looking for a date for this weekend (see Tiger Woods). But we're trying to help the needy, not the greedy.

For further sake of this example, let's say you belong to a social networking website like Facebook or MySpace. You're a popular person and you've got 200 online friends. These are all people in "your network." How would you go about finding a date among this group of people?

With one click, you can send an email to all 200 friends, asking them if they'd like to go to the movies with you on Saturday. But you're unlikely to do that. Even though a mass email gives you the greatest reach among your network, you intuitively know that a blanket message requesting a date isn't going to be welcomed by everyone. Before you select a potential partner, you're going to micro-segment your database.

First of all, you're going to eliminate all of the people in your network of the gender you *don't* want to date. In my case, it would be everyone of the male sex. You may decide this is a cross tab that you don't want to exclude one side or the other. As the Scarecrow told Dorothy, "Of course, people do go *both ways*."

Next you want to eliminate all your family members.* As fun as my Aunt Bertie is, she's not going to respond well to a romantic invitation to the cinema from me. Your message is wasted on your relatives.

Because you're an upstanding individual – and because of several mandatory training seminars from HR – you are not going to ask out any of your co-workers. So again, you ask the website to remove all your co-workers from the list.

By now, your network of 200 friends is considerably smaller. Maybe you've got forty or so candidates who are still in the running. You may micro-segment further. You've never been able to live down what happened to you freshman year at the pep rally, so remove all your old high school friends. There was an embarrassing hazing incident in college, so all those people come off the list too (at least the eyewitnesses). At some point, you might decide that your date would also have to be single, so eliminate all the married people†. You want someone local, so eliminate everyone outside of your zip code. And you're not interested

---

*   West Virginia joke goes here.

†   Divorcees are still okay. In fact, they might be a little desperate which works to your advantage.

in someone who's enrolled either in Medicare Part D or in 9th grade honors English, so set up some age parameters too*.

Now let's assume you're down to about fifteen people. As you scan the photographs of who is left, you will micro-segment even further. Either in your mind or on the screen, you're dropping people who have the wrong color hair, those who are too tall for you, or live with their mothers. You're keeping the ones who have a bright smile, a good sense of humor, a great job, superior wit, and a supermodel physique (a tall order for inside your zip code – but call me an optimist).

Ready, fire, aim

You'll keep going until you've whittled it down to one person, who you'll now ask out to the movies. Considering you started with 200 people, it may seem like cycling through all these preferences is a lot of trouble to locate only one person. But think about this: you already knew that 160 of them were people who would not find the content relevant (because they're already married to your sister or something). Deploying messaging to those 160 people would be a waste of your resources (even if it's only an email). You're also likely to offend a few of them...and you don't want to be confronted about your romantic email request by someone in the health club locker room.

This process-of-elimination exercise is a good example of how to most effectively conduct marketing in the 21st century. Sending a mass email to the network is just like running broadcast advertising, blanketing a neighborhood with direct mailing, or dropping leaflets from a helicopter. At least seventy-five to eighty percent of the message is wasted on people not in the market for what you're selling or highly unlikely to buy. The content is irrelevant and could hurt your chances of reaching them when you have a product offering that's not suited to their needs (like say a bachelor party or an Irish wake).

The other twenty percent of the network – the potential customers – are much more likely to be receptive to that message. Whether you're looking for just one person (like someone to date on Saturday) or you're hoping to grow a customer base (like a sultan starting a harem), this is the space in which you want to play. A targeted email to this group

---

* Coo-coo-ca-choo Mrs. Robinson.

(whether it's to forty opposite sex, unattached, non-relatives or to one smoking hottie) is more efficient than emailing everyone you know. Plus, you'll be able to measure the effectiveness of your marketing campaign based on the email replies you receive. You can also begin an ongoing dialogue with these potential customers, depending on how well the dinner conversation goes.

If all goes well, you'll soon be doing to the date what a number of AIG executives have been doing to their investors for years. If this is what effective micro-targeting and database segmentation can do for your social life, just think what it can do for your product!

Who are you?/I really want to know

Our goal in modern marketing is to find market segments that are predisposed to buying the product. You can't do that with traditional radio, television, or newspaper. They don't shoot with a sniper's scope; they shoot with a shotgun blast. While programming dayparts, station format, and specific publication can somewhat aim for a target market, mass media still often results in a ton of waste.

It's very important for all businesses to find out who their target market(s) is/are, quantify the market, then see what you can do as best as possible to segment your marketing efforts to these groups of consumers.

When talking about micro-segmentation, I joked that we could find you old ladies who live east of the river, drive blue cars, and have had cataract surgery and a penchant for mini-schnauzers. Why would that be important? Because maybe you run an ophthalmologist office on the west side of town and you're targeting potential patients for a new treatment of a condition that primarily affects the vision of elderly woman while they drive. (Does it really have to be *blue* cars then? No, but it could be luxury cars if the treatments are rather expensive, or women who drive used cars if patients are likely to get financial assistance for the treatment from the government. The dog? Well…there I'm just being plain silly. You *can* take it too far.)

Get on the list

How does the average marketer get a list of email addresses? The work can be tedious, but highly rewarding. You can purchase lists with dubious data from some third party. You can capture the addresses of web surfers who look at your website. But the best way is to have potential customers self-identify themselves by inviting them to sign up for newsletters, insider clubs, coupons, or contests online. These consumers are already likely to be your customers or will choose to "opt-in" in exchange for robust content which they find relevant. These consumers are ripe for growing into raving fans.

Your list is only as valuable as it is accurate. When people move, switch Internet providers, or get a new job, their email addresses often change. A large percentage – perhaps half – of the members of your online fan club will not re-enlist or will actively opt-out of the program*. Cleansing your database is an important maintenance routine, and just like getting your oil changed or seeing the dentist, it should be done on a regular basis (practicing good list hygiene is as important as flossing when it comes to maintaining a meaningful dialogue with customers).

Who invited you?

If your traditional customer is only looked at as Men 18-34 (or some other demographic) – and that's how you promote the product, position the product, base everything about marketing the product – you're not going to sell to a lot of people outside of that demo.

Working for Anheuser-Busch, I learned that at certain times of the year people who are not big beer drinkers may end up more likely drinking a brew. Summer picnics, playoff games, and holidays – these are all times when beer, wine, and spirits are important to the gathering. In addition to deploying messaging to the traditional young male beer-drinking demo, we would also deploy broadcast advertising to several expanded demos.

---

* Customers who die are labeled as having "involuntarily opted out of the program."

With more than 2,100 stores coast to coast, the local Home Depot is like Mecca to many testosterone-infused men who like power tools and lawn mowers. The Depot has done a great job of catering to the do-it-yourselfer, giving them the equipment and products to handle anything from building a deck to running in-wall speaker wire for surround sound. But it's not just the Tim Allen's of the world who shop there. There are many guys who don't know the business end of a hammer (like me), so they offer in-store experts to help the neophytes and to empower them to take on repair projects and upgrades*. The Home Depot attracts many female customers with products that appeal to them (like home décor or plants and gardening supplies) and free instructional classes to demonstrate the products and techniques required. Of course, the store is also a popular destination with professional contractors of all kinds.

Home Depot is hardware's version of Barnum's three-ring circus. There's something for everyone. So the chain deploys individualized content through different media channels, all in hopes of reaching each segment of their market. They're in the trade magazines, hoping to appeal to contractors. There's a different message they promote in TV commercials during football games, hoping to reach a different kind of customer. Of the 40,000 items in their store, the covers of their newspaper inserts feature – not drill bits and lumber – but full-color pictures of patio furniture, houseplants, and other home décor items. Each segment of their customer base is addressed through a different medium with targeted, relevant messaging. This is one of the reasons Home Depot is the 2nd largest retailer in the country, just behind Walmart.

I'm a little bit country store

The Walmart chain of stores has become the epicenter of many of the towns they sprout up in. Each Walmart seems to be bigger than the next, offering more kinds of products and services. They contain grocery stores, bank branches, optometry services, nail salons, portrait studios, sandwich shops, and burger joints – and that's just the outer perimeter of the store! Walmart is also introducing mini-clinics in stores staffed by nurse practitioners who can see patients on the spot and prescribe

---

*   Their slogan from 2003-2009: "You can do it. We can help."

medication to drive volume to their in store pharmacies, similar to the CVS Minute Clinic model. No lines, no waiting, and they accept most major insurance carriers. Never mind the thousands of items – from housewares and pet supplies to athletic shoes and electronics – among the aisles. Walmart could appropriate that Barnumesque quote about, "A seat for every ass and an ass in every seat."

The truth is Sam Walton didn't invent Walmart. It was invented by the wild, wild west. We called it the General Store and it was the one place pioneers and tenderfoots could get everything they needed. They'd drive the wagon into town and get their supplies for a week or more: hardware, perishables, horse feed, ammo. The country store is nearly as old as the country itself.

Isn't it interesting that we keep coming back to the concept of a "Superstore"? We have superstores for hardware, superstores for books and entertainment, and superstores for general merchandise. Malls are so 1980s! Who wants to go to a mall to do their shopping these days? There's no place to park. It has too many skateboarders. You have to walk past the massage chair salesman and the Dead Sea salt scrub salesman and the above-ground pool salesman just to get to the Food Court. Worst of all, they have the selection of stores that every other mall has. Blindfold me and drop me into a random mall and I'd have no way of knowing where I was. It'd be like waking up drunk in Levittown; all the houses look the same.

At the end of the day, every Walmart or Home Depot may look the same – but they're easy to shop in and they offer up pretty much anything to each and every customer who walks through their electronic sliding doors.

A needle with no thread

There is a bit of chicken and egg thing at play when trying to identify the target audience for any product. Every shoe designer must wonder, "Who will end up buying my designs? Upscale, fashion-conscious women? Or drag queens?" Hey, a buck is a buck – but it does make a difference as to what the model posing on the catalogue cover should look like.

Market segmenting doesn't need to be as broad as it is for Walmart or Home Depot. Like our social network hunt for a movie date, the market can be very narrow. If you want a tattoo, you *can't* get that at Walmart.* You have to go to a tattoo parlor. If you want a custom-made suit, you *can't* get that at Walmart. You have to go to a haberdashery or an upscale store like Brooks Brothers or Neiman Marcus.

That's not a bad thing. What is the customer profile of a typical shopper at Walmart versus a typical shopper at Neiman Marcus? They're on opposite ends of the spectrum — whatever spectrum you want to measure them against. Surely, a Neiman Marcus patron may find himself wandering the aisles at Walmart from time to time, but is he going to buy a suit at Walmart? Or jewelry? Most likely, not.

Thank you for your business

Credit cards run advantage promotions, soft drink makers run rewards programs, and airlines run frequent flier programs. These are all classic examples of customer loyalty programs. They've been used by businesses for more than 100 years as a way of rewarding and retaining customers. But today these programs can be the single most powerful tool for marketers — even more effective than television, newspaper, or web banners.

Take a look at our work with state lotteries. What segment of the market plays the lottery? For years, it's been hard to pin down the answer to that because buying a scratch ticket is a pretty anonymous purchase. But based on a lot of anecdotal evidence (people we see buying the tickets, people who show up to claim the prizes) we've thought for years that most lottery players were senior citizens and working-class people dreaming of a big payday.

In 2006, our company launched a customer loyalty program for state lotteries called Lottery Replay!®. This platform allowed players to take their non-winning† tickets and get a second chance at winning prizes on the Internet. By entering a serial code on the back of the ticket, players could either win an instant prize (like a gift certificate for an oil change) or win points which can be accumulated and applied toward chances to

---

* You'll *see* a lot of them at Walmart, but you can't buy them there.

† This sounds *way* nicer than "losing tickets."

win larger prizes (like gift certificates to restaurants or overnight stays at resorts). The marketing partners (the restaurants, the hotels, and the rest) get a heavy dose of exposure. The players get additional value to their tickets without changing the price point. The lottery gets a whole database of people who "opt-in" to accumulate points and continue their play experience online and outside the traditional retail distribution channel. Players are no longer faceless, nameless, anonymous people (except those who win a billion dollars). Using the web, the players are now *addressable*. The lottery now has a "network" of raving fans to which they can deploy relevant and segmented content.

But it goes way beyond just building a database of email addresses. By opting in, players give a small amount of demographic information. If the lottery rewards players with additional points, they tell a little bit more about themselves. They may take online surveys. They may indicate what products they have preferences for and which they don't. Now this network can be micro-segmented. And this powerful list of consumers has potent value to anyone who sells products by way of gas stations and convenience stores.

What did the Lottery's use of Replay!® reveal about their network? Without giving away any proprietary information, let's just say they discovered things no other state lottery ever knew. Their demo was broader and primarily younger than they presumed; the players were better educated and earned more money than previously believed. As each entry code is unique, it is easy to see who is buying and replaying which tickets. They can see which demos liked the jackpot games, which preferred the instant games. They could further see who was buying $1.00 tickets and who was buying $20.00 tickets. This was invaluable information needed to make decisions about what kinds of new lottery products would do well and which could use additional marketing support. For example, the lottery began selling tickets that had prizes which would appeal to the younger demographic: things like tickets to sporting events, mp3 downloads, and motorcycles[*]. Could this demographic data be skewed by the fact that Lottery Replay!® players

---

[*] This is not to say that older demos wouldn't like to win a prize like a motorcycle or a seat at a ball game. I did have to scratch my head when my mother tried to win a free mp3 to download. She doesn't own an iPod and hasn't listened to what she considers "contemporary music" since 1962.

need to own a computer and an Internet connection, unlike lottery players who just need a ticket? Perhaps. But even if there are some flaws in the data, there is enough there for true marketing innovations. The fact is the widespread use of home computers and handheld mobile devices is growing every day – from kids to seniors. In 2008, 231 million Americans were internet users, second only to China.

This way to the Egress

For 25 cents anyone could enter P.T. Barnum's American Museum. It was filled with all sorts of curiosities – "genuine fakes" – including General Tom Thumb and the Fiji mermaid (actually a monkey's torso sewn on to the back of a fish). So naturally, visitors were intrigued by the prominent signs pointing "this way to the Egress." What mysterious creature could this be? Those who didn't know that "egress" was another word for "exit" found themselves walking out to the street through a door that locked behind them. Anyone who wanted to come back in had to pay another quarter.

If P.T. Barnum were around today, he wouldn't be tricking you to go out; he'd be tricking you to "opt in." He'd be finding a way to obtain email addresses and SMS numbers for everyone who came to the circus or visited the museum[*]. He would create a database of everyone who ever visited the Big Top. He'd ask them about which acts they enjoyed the most. Those people who said "the clowns" would very likely receive clown-themed emails[†]. Those who liked the animal acts would get messages about Jumbo and the lion tamers. Those who enjoyed the acrobats would get emails with video embedded of trapeze artists and tightrope walkers. All designed to appeal specifically to the precise tastes of Barnum's customers in an effort to be sure they came back to "The Greatest Show on Earth" again and again.

Barnum would have the database segmented into neighborhoods and alert fans along the route when the circus train would be coming through their town. The database would be segmented into cities and

---

[*] But knowing Barnum he'd probably do it in some colorful way, like sending emails that say "prescription drugs cheap" or "enhance her pleasure."

[†] Actually, it would be one medium-sized email and 67 clown emails would jump out of it.

zip codes so Barnum could give advanced notice to those geographic areas. He would text message special rates to those in his network and offer exclusive meet-and-greet events with circus performers (segmented by fan preference). He would deploy electronic coupons that fans could forward to their friends, allowing Barnum to obtain their friends' email addresses too. There would be customer loyalty programs allowing circus patrons to earn points for special events or priority seating.

You don't have to be a great showman to build a network and know how to divide it up to suit customer preferences.

Historians debate whether Barnum actually said the quote most attributed to him: "There's a sucker born every minute." Barnum actually considered the American public to be quite savvy. P.T. Barnum *did* make one quote which still holds true, especial in today's digital world. He said, "Every crowd has a silver lining."

Chapter seven

My Content on My Terms

Why TV, radio, newspapers, and traditional gatekeepers no longer matter

As a species, we are addicted to content.

No, we don't think of it that way. Most of us don't think of the things we consume – news reports, popular music, office gossip, someone's last tweet – as "content." But we constantly are taking in and processing content. It can be for education, entertainment, or for self-preservation.[*] We are sated by its absorption. We impress others with its regurgitation. We sound smarter at cocktail parties discussing foreign policy. We appear wiser at ball games rattling off batting averages, ERAs, and box scores. We seem sexier to other disco dancers when we can guess their signs and read their aura.

What's different in today's world is we no longer consume content only at breakfast, lunch, and dinner. We have a D5W IV drip of information plugged directly into out bodies for round-the-clock consumption and nourishment.

---

[*] Oh sure, you're jaded now because you've heard it a million times and you want to seem cool…but the first time you were on a plane, you *listened* to that safety procedures demonstration and looked around for the exit over the wing. Now, you don't even bother to check for a clean barf bag.

Can we talk?

The naked ape has always found ways to communicate. The cave man used hand signals and grunts to pass information to each other[*]. They created cave paintings. The Egyptians made hieroglyphics; the Indians had smoke signals. There are tribes on the subcontinent that still communicate with tongue clicks, whistles, and calls.

The Greeks and Romans developed their alphabets and the spoken word could be preserved in stone or on parchment. Ships have depended on lighthouses since before the birth of Christ. After the Dark Ages, stained glass windows in cathedrals taught the illiterate about religion, history, morality, and contemporary politics.

When Johannes Gutenberg made his contraption in 1455, the thirst for content – not mere information – was born. It was like adding vodka to orange juice or frothy milk to coffee: no longer something you needed to survive, but something you wanted to improve your quality of life.

Gutenberg's Bible might as well have been bound in hand-blown glass, because it was like a crack pipe for content. He didn't dress like Huggy Bear on "Starsky and Hutch," but Gutenberg was the world's first content pusher. Once people took a hit, they were hooked and gave birth to generations of content-craving crack babies.

My content

The span of time between content innovations gets shorter and shorter. Between Gutenberg and the revival of theater, the growth of the broadsheet newspaper and the popular novel, the invention of the telegraph and the telephone, the development of radio and television, less time passes between each revolution. We had 70 years of vinyl records, 20 years of CD's, and so far about 10 years of mp3's[†]. We've had the iPod for less than a decade and we've already evolved to portable music players in our phones (and phones in our portable music players). The kid who enters high school next year will likely be listening to

---

[*] Such as asking, "Does this woolly mammoth-hide pant suit make my ass look fat?"

[†] There were also a couple of years of 8-tracks and cassettes in there, but I'm trying my best to forget the '70s.

their favorite tunes on a completely new platform by the time they graduate.

Advancing technology and the consumer's desire to utilize these toys means the traditional way in which we view content is no longer the rule. We have access to more content in more ways on more platforms than ever before. "I want it now." "I want to pause it." "I want it in Spanish." "I want it sent to my phone." "I want to see graphics." "I want additional information on the topic." "I want to participate in the judging." "I want to skip the commercials!"

Few of us would think of ourselves as more privileged than a Rockefeller, living a life more powerful than a king or more decadent that a sultan. Consider this. No matter what your family pedigree, right now you can:

- Have access anytime you want to the most prestigious symphonies playing the greatest classical music in the world!
- View every masterpiece and *objet d'art* in any museum on any continent.
- Hold command performances by your favorite actors of dramas, comedies, and Broadway musicals.
- Browse the research of the greatest libraries and institutions of higher learning at a fraction of the time.
- Consider the works and views of the greatest thinkers, leaders, authors, and artists of this age or any other.
- Instantly have access to breaking news as it happens, unedited, unfiltered, and un-editorialized.
- Instantaneously retrieve virtually all of the knowledge in the known world.
- Do all of these things on demand, day or night, from your home, your office, or nearly anywhere else you go.

My terms

There's no question that the quantity of content has exploded; this isn't something that was unforeseen. The major shift (and the one that has the biggest impact on advertising) is in the terms of use. My content has gotten deeper, but the terms of when and how I use it are now unlike anything ever before.

The questions I ask myself today about "my terms" regarding content are:

- When am I going to consume it?
- Where am I going to consume it?
- How attentive will I be when I consume it?

For most of the past five decades, we've had little choice other than to watch the TV in the living room or family room. Although we've had VCR's since the mid-1970s, the great majority of our viewing was done in real-time. We still love the television because it's usually bigger and brighter than a computer screen (especially if we're talking about HDTV) and we use it while sitting on a comfy sofa, not some folding chair and a card table. Plus, there aren't a lot of buttons to press to operate a TV*. The DVR is extremely facile for skipping content.

Now we can watch an episode of "The Simpsons" from last Sunday or from 1995 on our tiny laptops or even tinier Smartphones. What we don't get in picture size and resolution we make up for in mobility and control. Like fast food, we've exchanged quality for convenience (although, it's hard to argue that picture quality for Smartphones doesn't get better and better each year; you can't say *that* about a Big Mac). I'm convinced that my high school and college-aged sons could watch a 10 hour mini-series on an iPhone and have little or no problem enjoying and appreciating every second. Maybe size doesn't matter?

---

* You never really take notice of how many buttons there are on your remote controls until you try to leave an elderly relative in your living room with your home entertainment system. Personally, I don't see the big mystery in needing to turn the cable box on before the TV or swapping the video and audio sources if you decide to watch a DVD. But some of my relatives look at me like I asked them to crack the da Vinci Code when I tell them why the volume isn't going down even though they're pressing the button.

Why stay up late to watch Letterman when you can hear a podcast of his Top Ten List when you get to work? Urban commuters – at least those that don't have to sit behind a wheel and drive – are using their time on buses and subways to get caught up on their prime time sitcoms. Or they save themselves ten minutes of their morning routine by getting the news headlines after they've already left the house. Before you can check who finally won that extra-inning West Coast night game in the paper or on your computer, the score has already been texted to your phone. If you prefer your morning content from TV in the car, you can simply get it from your favorite Fox News babe on Sirius/XM satellite radio or any number of other near-commercial free channels simulcast from television.

The great variable with watching, listening, or reading content "on my terms" is the question of just how much content will be absorbed. The attention level to a podcast when jogging a quiet neighborhood is different than when sitting on a crowded subway or sneaking a peek from your office desktop. It's just like the problem radio stations have: most of the people using the medium are doing something else (see *driving*).

You are the gatekeeper

One of the reasons that TV, radio, and newspapers no longer matter much is that the nicotine-stained fingers of the men and women in those editorial meetings, deciding the importance of events from their Ivory Towers, aren't the only gatekeepers of information anymore. In fact, they're not even part of the conversation. Newspapers have finally become the "post game show" of modern communications (*more on this to come…*). At one time, publishers, editors, and writers of newspaper content were the ones who separated the wheat from the chaff, examining the grand scope of incoming news content and deciding which was worthy of broadcast/publication. So much content is disseminated these days that no one can vet all of it. The average person has access – in real time – to most of the same original news sources and data streams of raw information those editors have (without the deadlines). Today's news consumer can pick and choose which stories they read by sheer whim or by pre-determined keyword*.

For all of us in a social network, we're not only reading the news but passing along news too. If you have a blog, a website, a Twitter feed, or a MySpace page, congratulations; you are a gatekeeper. You decide what content gets passed to your personal network. If your local paper doesn't carry the story about your chowder society mixer, you can post photos on your website. Whether it's an article on a political candidate, a book review, or a home video of a cat operating a salad shooter, you can forward content you get from other websites to your network (who needs a Woodward or a Bernstein?)

By definition and by practice, that makes us all gatekeepers too. Not every online joke we hear is forwarded to everyone in our address book†. Whether we tweet content that furthers our agendas or just says something about our personalities and experiences, we are deciding what gets through the gate. When members of our network re-tweet the content to their networks – and so on – we can watch the information go viral.

Stop the presses!

A wise man once said, "If the T-rex knew he was going to become extinct, then he wouldn't have." It's simple Darwinism to proclaim that species which can adapt will survive, and the ones that don't try to survive – the ones who don't realize their survival is in peril – will perish‡. It is survival of the "fittest," not the "fastest," "strongest," or "smartest."

---

*   Such as "bikini tragedy."

†   Did you hear that, Uncle Bernie? You don't have to send me *every single guy-walks-into-a-bar joke* that your squash partner shoots your way. They're not all that funny. And even if they were, why would I want to read the same ones seven times a day? And, by the way, can you ask Aunt Mary June to stop forwarding me all those chain letters? For the last time, some kid in Oregon is *not* going to get a kidney transplant if the email is forwarded to just 20 more people.

‡   This philosophy doesn't take into account the chance that the dinosaurs were killed by an asteroid striking the earth and wrecking the planet's ecosystem. I mean, even if you *know* that's going to happen, there's only so much you can do about it. So the dinosaurs were pretty much screwed.

I have a friend who runs a newspaper. When we talk in broad terms about what he does, he likes to say, "I'm in the newspaper business..." He simply doesn't get it. He's not in the "newspaper" business; he's in the "content delivery" business. Until he embraces that the fundamental concept, the essence of what he does – that his enterprise is based on the words his people write, not the ink-stained paper on which those words are served – he's headed to the prom in a dinosaur tuxedo.

Content is king. It always has been. Gutenberg didn't make the Bible better; he just made it easier for people to read it. The radio didn't make Sinatra sing better; it just brought his songs to the masses. Surely, sometimes the medium affects the message (a majority of those who watched the 1960 Nixon/Kennedy debates on television thought the charismatic Massachusetts Senator won; those who listened to the debate on the radio were won over by Nixon, who TV viewers perceived optically as sweaty and unshaven). Not all content is *quality* content – think of the series of YouTube videos of people dancing poorly to Michael Jackson's "Thriller" or dilettantes who watch "Gilligan's Island" re-runs on their $5,000 HDTVs – but it's the promise of relevant content delivery that makes folks jettison their books for Kindles or their CD players for iPods.

Great journalism will always be appreciated by those who seek it. Our society will always be better for the free and open exchange of ideas. But just as we've moved off the soap box in the town square to the editorial page, that discussion is again moving to new digs. Are there people out there who insist on a hardcopy newspaper each day and will not purchase an IBM-clone just to read their horoscopes? Sure there are – a dwindling number of them, but a number of people nonetheless (Information age? I know people who still don't have *cable TV!*). Reading a paper has been a cultural habit for several generations of Americans, and one that they enjoy. A paper is far more convenient for taking on a vacation or into the bathroom. And you can't wrap yesterday's fish or line a bird cage with a Dell.[*]

The critical knock on newspapers is they waste an awful lot of natural resources. Today there's a tremendous backlash against those who squander money and resources[†]. The average home newspaper

---

[*] Although I know several IT guys who would argue the point.

[†] It should be worth noting that the book you hold in your hands (if you are in-

subscription creates 550 pounds of refuse a year. The daily production of newsprint kills lots of trees, uses a ton of electricity to operate the presses, creates industrial sludge from the ink, and burns off millions of gallons of gas to deliver to newsstands and mailboxes from coast-to-coast. Not to mention the union salaries of all those pressmen and circulation coordinators who produce the final printed product. But the fatal flaw in the modern newspaper is that by the time it lands on your front porch (or in my case, the rhododendron bush), the news they printed several hours before is painfully out of date.

In the last two years, more than a dozen major daily papers have closed (including the *Rocky Mountain News*, the *Baltimore Examiner*, and the *Cincinnati Post*) and *Time* magazine has predicted the imminent downfall or digitalization of 10 more (including the *Boston Globe*, the *NY Daily News*, the *Chicago Sun-Times*, the *Miami Herald*, and the *San Francisco Chronicle*)*.

For those publishers who are keeping their presses going because of sentimentality or to serve an ever-dwindling percentage of the population that can't get their news another away, the End of Days is nigh!

Waiting for the end of the world

There are those who love the way Glenn Miller played songs that made the Hit Parade, and who think web-enabled cell phones are expensive toys for indulgent meatheads. Even though them's fightin' words, there's no use getting into an argument with these people about whether newspapers will cease to exist. It's like worrying about whether the sun will burn out in 4.5 or in 5 billion years. *Why do YOU care? You're not going to be around to see it.*

---

deed holding this content in the form of a hardcopy and not on a digital platform) is produced using sustainable publishing practices. Chief among them is that my publisher can produce books on demand - fulfill store requests to order for 5 or 20 or 100 copies – which eliminates the need for large print runs, saves paper, and minimizes waste. I have reported this practice to Al Gore in hopes of an "atta-boy," but still haven't heard from him.

* Interesting that *Time* magazine is opining about the eminent demise of newspapers. The very same technology that's killing off the newspaper business has had the same effect on magazines. *Time* doesn't have much……

The key is this: newspapers have become to news what the Pony Express has become to shipping. Consumers will not "opt-in" to dated content that's stale before they open it. Besides, it's so much easier to click on one's laptop (or iPhone or Kindle) while drinking a cup of coffee versus searching through the rhododendron bush at my house trying to the find the paper!

What exactly do the End of Days look like for newspapers? Something quite like what we're seeing each and every day: dailies becoming weeklies, weeklies becoming monthlies, and many of the rest folding all together. For a time there will be reporters and editors with tin cups selling pencils on street corners; there will be fewer organizations paying journalists to create content for distribution via an arcane and irrelevant medium.

Whoever is left when the brimstone settles on the streets will huddle together and create a new infrastructure for delivery. Much like the locally-owned TV station is affiliated with a network, "papers" will pool resources to more efficiently deliver strong, relevant content – in a new way.

Again, it will become survival of "the fittest," not the "flashiest," not the "best-written," or even the "most profitable." Hardcopy newspapers will exist as novelties in some areas. Niche publications like penny savers and shopper's guides might continue if they can keep their overhead low, while still containing community micro-segmented content (whose kid made the honor roll, what the local little league team is up to, the giant pothole at Lake and Pine Streets that shredded my Michelins). Newspaper "publishers" will instead push content on the web or in mobile phone apps. With no set printing time, the "deadline" will be a thing of the past. Once content is created (and hopefully, properly vetted) it will be posted. The great difference between newsprint scribes and between the online news content creators of today is that online reporters may not wait until all their sources call back before running the story. Every enterprise story will evolve in real time receiving updates and connections just as breaking news stories do.

For example, a business story about a hike in interest rates would start with an immediate posting that the Fed has raised rates. Instead of getting reaction from several economists before publishing further, the online reporter would "update" the original dispatch with quotes from the first economist that called her back. Each time a source would weigh in, the dispatch would be updated. When the Dow Jones takes a nose dive at lunch because of the rate hike, the reporter would continue to reshape the original story. The story continues to build, so stay tuned! Content drives the story, the story drives more content!

The reporter of the future will not put her pencil down or push her keyboard under her desk once the story has been filed. She will continue to add more, enticing people to come back and look for updates. She will engage those commenting on the news, even use the reader comments to further the story. The story will develop and unfold in real time – *that's* dynamic content!

Brother, can you make a dime?

Can they monetize the news on the Internet? Don't ask Rupert Murdock if it's easy to do. He found it was hard to convince people to pay for content they've been getting for free (and can still get free at other websites). Instead, ask Hugh Hefner. Anyone who can Google can find pornography for free on the Internet. So why do some people have paid subscriptions to Playboy.com? It's because Hef's website offers premium content not available elsewhere.

"Newspapers" can still offer premium content online in the form of in-depth reports, investigative series, or commentary from popular, well-respected writers. Just as people ponied up the monthly fees to listen to Howard Stern on Sirius/XM satellite radio, there are plenty of people who would pay a small fee to read Pat Buchanan, Dear Abby, or Dave Berry.

Will they make more money on fees than they did when print was king? No. (*Playboy*'s subscriptions are declining like every other magazine's; the web content value is not enough to offset all those losses.) But as print's days are numbered – and the forests think it isn't happening a moment too soon – those publishers who become media agnostic and distribute their content on a number of platforms will live to see the sun rise again.

Cold turkey

There's no telling what kind of content will have value in the coming years. But it will affect – and be affected by – the kinds of media platforms that will be available. TV programs with live Twitter feeds for running commentary. Video players with one-touch voting abilities (who needs a *second* night of ballad singers or bossa nova dancers?). Don't just "call in" to Larry King, "Skype in" and become a virtual guest[*].

This is certain to happen because we remain addicted to timely content. There is no sea change of public behavior conceivable that would reverse that. Granted, we may not exactly be at the point where we walk around with IV's of data dripping into our veins (data is already dripping into the Smartphones in our back pockets), but we're getting close. Don't believe me? Try going cold turkey on content for a couple of hours. No books. No cell phones. No TV. No Internet. No news. No tweets. No texts. No IMing. No email. No voicemail. You'll see. After a few hours you'll start sweating like a junkie, calling out for Huggy Bear, desperately needing a fix.

---

[*] "Caller, what's your question?"

Chapter eight

Opting Out

The DVR is older than television itself

One of the finest improvements to television viewing has been the invention of the digital video recorder, or, DVR. Pioneered by TiVo, it has gone far beyond a replacement device for the VCR. Its ease of use in combining high quality recording and playback with channel listings information has radically changed the way most of us use the television.

The feature that captured our imaginations – and rewired the way we perceive a broadcast – is the ability to control, pause, and rewind live TV. For those of us under its spell, the DVR has removed all urgency from programming. We miss *nothing*. We can stop the action of a football game, a sitcom, or the evening news at a whim. When we decide something else is more important to us than the content we're consuming[*], we simply pause.

But truth be told the DVR has been around since before the first television broadcast, since before the first radio broadcast. We have a biological DVR: it's called our bladder. The pressure exuded by that organ when it's full forces us to decide: *Do I want to continue consuming this content or do I want to go to the bathroom?* If the content is really compelling (like an extra-inning rally, a breaking news story, or a detective about to reveal the murderer) then we might choose to tough it out. We stick with it until we decide that the content we're consuming

---

[*] Something like the phone ringing, a baby crying, or a cat scratching the legs of an antique table.

is no longer more important than taking a whiz. And what content do we often find irrelevant, unentertaining, or unable to otherwise hold our attention? The commercials!

Our bladders (our biological DVR's) have trained us to triage the value of the content we get and choose when to "opt out." And opting out is the wave of the future.

Let's do the time shift again

The threat of DVR use to commercial television is self-evident. The device can skim past commercial content (or any other linear content we don't want) with an ease and sophistication previously unseen. The idea of time-shifting through commercials was a fringe benefit to most VCR owners (they wanted a tape machine so they could record "Falcon Crest" back in the '80s when they weren't home). But the DVR generation wants the functionality of manipulating the playback of *all* their TV content. And they're willing to pay for it.

More and more consumers are opting out of advertising. The practice is called "paid avoidance." Instead of accepting that sponsorships are a natural byproduct of programming, we're seeing them as being in the way. According to a 2009 study by Synovate, eighty-seven percent of those surveyed have actively tried to avoid TV and radio advertising by turning off, changing channels, or using personal video recorders to fast-forward through recorded ads. True, we've *always* had a distain for a used-car commercial popping up just as the evil twin[*] walks back into the soap opera heroine's life after being missing in the Andes for seven years. The difference is today we are *empowered* to do something about it. We can zap the commercial. Sure, we could still use a VCR for almost no additional cost. But we are willing to pay TiVo or the cable company a little extra each month so we can have the option of watching commercial television in real time without the commercials. Hence, the End of Days is clearly nearing for network television based on advertising revenues to pay for programming.

---

[*]   Roberto

Pay TV or not Pay TV?

What's also different now is that with the multitude of platforms to view content comes a multitude of pay models for funding that content. We can get free television broadcasts by watching the programs network sponsors have paid for. The cost to us: sixteen minutes each hour of having to view the commercials. For many of us, that kind of "free" is simply too expensive. We'd rather pay a few bucks and get those minutes back (or to just not be bothered). So we download the latest episode of "Glee" from iTunes or pay the cable company a premium for a DVR to zap the ads while we watch.

We also have the option of watching television without commercials. HBO and Showtime have proven that people will pay for premium television content. An "Entourage" viewer or fan of "Californication" is able to opt out of advertising simply by paying for the channels. The premium channels — which can also exercise artistic choices unbound by commercial broadcast regulation — offer a product that the average viewer is willing to shell out a few extra bucks for.

Fans have demonstrated they are willing to pay for copies of commercial-free episodes of their favorite series on DVD or Blu-ray. Videoscan reported in 2004 that the ratings-starved (but cult-favorite) "Chappelle's Show" became the all-time best-selling TV show on DVD[*], surpassing "The Simpsons." In fact, DVD sales of the then-defunct "Family Guy" were so robust that Fox TV resurrected the show for broadcast in 2005, three years after cancelling it. Today, it's standard practice to release a boxed set of a show's complete season right after the May cliffhanger — just in time for holiday gift giving!

In many ways, this commercial model is already at work successfully in noncommercial broadcasting. Look at PBS (the Public Broadcasting System) and your local public broadcaster. They offer specialized programming that viewers (or, "members") will watch after sitting through a number of pledge breaks and membership drives. For some of us, that's a reasonable price to pay in order to view a Ken Burns documentary (for some of us, we'd rather swallow broken glass than watch 37 hours of black & white still photos of fly fishing).

---

[*] "I'm Rick James, bitch."

Who would have thought that National Public Radio (NPR) and PBS would be the best contemporary examples of a subscription media model? It's a great illustration of active participatory programming. While they don't directly buy a subscription to NPR or PBS, their audiences opt in to the content. They become "members" and are rabid fans of the programming, whether it's *All Things Considered*, *A Prairie Home Companion,* or my personal favorite *Wait Wait, Don't Tell Me* (who wouldn't want Carl Castle's voice on their home answering machine?). Not only do they support NPR and PBS with their checkbooks (which they clearly don't have to), they are motivated, articulate evangelists who have bought into public broadcasting's exported culture. How else do you explain all those tote bags?

The mirror has two faces

In this new age of consumer pragmatism, no one wants to pay for things they don't need (as opposed to paying for the things they don't want). Whether it's the extended warranty on a laptop, the "Simonizing" of a new car or the stain protection on a new couch, we'll likely resist.

When I sit down in an upscale New York restaurant, why must the waiter inquire if I'll be drinking "bottled" water? I'm insulted that they even ask. Do I look like I'd rather pay extra for something that I should be getting for free? Very few people I know have died from drinking the water in Manhattan; it may not be perfect but it's not Calcutta. "No, I'll be having tap[*]," I say with as much indignation as I can muster. I don't mind paying for things I believe have value. Bottled water is not one of them.

However, if I'm going to Acapulco, I might consider smuggling in several canteens of water like Gunga Din for the sole purpose of making ice for my margaritas. In fact, I'm likely to spend so much more on an unopened bottle of water that it would be cheaper for me actually to brush my teeth with tequila[†].

---

[*] To this day when many New Yorkers order tap instead of Evian, they ask for the "Giuliani." This is a wink to the former mayor's effort to clean up the potable water supply.

[†] Not recommended by the American Dental Association.

Yes, people will pay to avoid things objectionable to them. But, they are also willing to pay for something if it has a sufficient enough value to them at a given time, place, or circumstance.

Although we generally detest sitting through a three minute block of boring commercials, many of us *are* willing to watch one 15-second ad before viewing a video clip on AOL. We consider that 15 seconds a fair trade – especially if it's an entertaining, compelling, or an otherwise relevant 15 seconds – for being able to view the content we've determined is relevant to us on our desktop at work or our Droid on the bus. Most prime time shows can be viewed on the networks' websites at the cost of running one or two commercials (as opposed to a full complement or "blocks" of ads in a 30 or 60 minute series). Viewers are increasingly taking advantage because they believe the amount of sponsorship interruption is reasonable given the access and convenience and the personal relevance of the content available on demand. Advertisers are taking advantage because there is much less message waste and viewers can't fast-forward through the spots if they want the content to which they have already elected to "opt in." Remember too these viewers have self-selected their interest. They want to know what's on the other side of a 15 second web ad. In their minds, by today's standards, it's a fair and equitable trade.

Just sit through our one-hour presentation…

Consumers will pay to avoid seeing the sales pitch, but will they ever choose to take the sales pitch in order to get content for free? Fortunately for advertisers, the answer is sometimes almost unbelievably…yes!

My parents are among the worst offenders of sitting through some sales presentation for a time-share in order to get a free tchotchke. "Here's a free lunch if we can discuss your financial planning." "Let us tell you about our condos, and you'll get day passes to Walt Disney World*." "We'll fly you in for a complimentary weekend at our resort if we can just get you alone in a room for an hour and not let you leave until you've heard what we have to say."

---

* My parents *already* have a condo in Florida. My father hates long lines – thus hates Walt Disney World.

It's a horrible, horrible way to make a hard sale (and I'm relieved to know whatever ring of Hell I'm eventually banished to for my contribution to media manipulation of the masses through the advertising I've created over the years, that I'll still be able to look down at these shysters in the ring below me). Despite its execution in those examples, there is something prudent about the concept.

We pay nearly $10 a head to get in to see a movie ($12 if you're living in LA or seeing something with those pesky 3D glasses in IMAX), more than twice that much to see a local live theater production. What if an advertiser offered you free admission? All you had to do was sit through their commercials before the show and during intermission. Would you do it? You already tolerate – in some cases, look forward to – advertising in the form of film trailers*. I'm guessing your answer is "Yes I'd take the free admission…depending on the show and amount of advertising I'd be subjecting myself to."

This is the value proposition: could it work if demand for the show were high enough to create a balance with the appropriate amount of messaging? Those interested in seeing a film-revival of "Casablanca" on the big screen might be first willing to sit through a two-minute speech from the local banker who sponsored the show. Given the option of seeing a midnight premier of "Harry Potter 7" if they'd only view a lengthy infomercial by Old Navy, most fans would aparate to an alternative theater where they could just pay the admission. For its part, Old Navy would probably feel subsidizing a $70 million box office bill would require so many commercials and in-product placements that the film would need to be re-titled "Harry Potter and the Half-Zip Fleece."

This model is intriguing. It might work on a small, affordable scale but not on worldwide distribution. Even in the movie theater, people can still opt out. They take their biological DVR (bladder) with them everywhere (or their iPhone, or cell phone, or…).

---

* Whenever I'm at the movies and instead of a preview I get a cinematic Coca-Cola commercial, I feel ripped off. I paid an arm-and-a-leg for a ticket, a tub of popcorn, and a splash of butter-flavored soy product (which according to the AMA will definitely harden my arteries). I feel like my admission already has been *paid*. So why am I watching a Coke commercial? Besides, I already purchased a $6.00 30 oz Diet Coke with the popcorn, and the last thing I need is *more*. When I come in, what I really wish I had during the movie is a urinal.

What's it all about, Alfie?

So what's the up-side to the number of media consumers opting out?

For one thing, there's no free lunch. Quality content cannot be created in any mass quantity without some kind of funding. While some forms of entertainment are theoretically self-sustaining (like HBO dramas paid for by subscription fees instead of commercial breaks), most need the free market to exist. This is not a bad thing; even da Vinci had patrons.

You can watch people fall off of skateboards for free for hours on YouTube, but companies are paying for space in the banners too. There will always be producers looking for advertisers, big and small, local and national, to support their work. If buying a 30 second ad during the broadcast season finale of "Lost" is too expensive (or is wasted on too many people that will never use your product or service, or who will DVR through your commercial), perhaps you can purchase banner ads or video teasers for the "Lost" web rebroadcast that deploy only for people in certain geographic or demographic micro-segmented cross-tabs.

There are opportunities for product placement in the majority of programs. No fictional character will ever again walk into a bar and order simply "a beer." The firefighters on "Rescue Me" drink Samuel Adams in front of neon Sam Adams signs, the fun-loving frat guys of the movie "Knocked Up" were always asking for Coronas and holding the bottles at *just* the correct angle, and how about the guys on "Entourage?" They are all Bud Men (nice to see Vince Chase, Johnny Drama, and the Turtle are men of good taste). Even if you're not a mega-corporation like Coca-Cola and can't get frosty glasses of your beverage in front of Simon, Randy, Kara, and Ellen, there are other options. A haberdashery gets its suits on the anchors of the local news in exchange for promotional mentions or credit. A hospital can market itself by sponsoring a medical information minute (and likely create the content and proffer talent from their in-house staff of medical experts over the web).

The technical ability to get past the extraneous content on TV is self-evident. More and more brand names, iconic labels, and product demonstrations will find their way into the storylines – the most desirable content – of the programming. All the coolest TV detectives will call the morgue on the latest flip phones. Desperate Housewives will drive the SUVs of their lead automotive sponsor. More scenes on sitcoms and family dramas will happen in the kitchens, where virtually any product could appear on the counter behind them[*]. Nothing makes you want a Country Time Lemonade more than watching a dozen reality-show castaways chug it down for dear life. One minute a trainer on "The Biggest Loser" will be encouraging a morbidly obese contestant to hit the treadmill; the next minute they'll be giving him a "lesson" about the benefits of low-fat Quaker Instant Oatmeal (never mind…they do that already).

It won't be just the products themselves. More of the real estate of your TV screen will be covered with logos for commercial products. The game clock or digital scoreboard will continue to feature an airline's logo right next to the team's logo. Among the chattering, flashing, scrolling mess of metadata bombarding the margins of morning talk show broadcasts, products and their labels will float by between national headlines and the drive-time weather. Just try to concentrate on the CNBC screen for more than ten seconds. The networks' years of self-promotion – having graphics and teasers for other shows push onto the screen to silently interrupt the action at rise – have begun to inoculate us to this kind of marketing. It won't be long before those promos for "Law and Order" which pop up in the middle of "30 Rock" are replaced with ads for Planter's mixed nuts and Coco-Puffs – ads impossible to DVR around.

Another positive thing: the compressed time has spawned a new wave of creativity for those making streaming video ads (we can't in good conscience call them "television" ads today) for new digital platforms. The need to make the clips only 10 or 15 seconds has forced advertisers to re-think the cookie-cutter creative approach they've been using

---

[*] Or for that matter, any product could appear *virtually*. The same technology that superimposes green-screen billboards behind home plate can insert a bottle of Pepsi or a box of Rice-a-Roni into a TV show. Technically, we can now make 1970s shows in syndication like "Rhoda," "Maude," or "Chico and the Man" serve Tyson chicken nuggets to their families 15 years before chicken nuggets are even invented.

these many years. Most streaming ads are snappier, quicker. There's no waiting around for a punch line; they sock it to you right away. I repeat: advertising *itself* doesn't suck; the way most people continue to practice it *does*. The necessity of making shorter commercials has made many of them better.

And the dinosaurs? They'll soon be gone and archaeologists will spend years combing over the remains of what once were modern newspaper presses, viewing them much like we now view the skeletal remains of the pre-historic giants who once roamed the Earth at the top of the food chain.

Chapter nine

Branding Should Only Happen to Cattle

The battle for hearts and minds

The most overused word in the advertising and marketing business today is "branding*." Everybody wants to do something with their brand. They want to update the brand. They want to freshen up the brand. They want to build the brand. They want to reposition the brand. They want to scrap the brand and start all over. They look at brand identity, brand name, brand personality, brand equity, and brand value.

They like to jiggle with the name, rework the logo art, and tinker with the label and even the recipe. They add "new and improved" to the box. They try to place the product in new situations with new audiences hoping to create a new image. All in the name of building a better brand. Let's face it: no matter how much you improve the package, a Pop Tart still tastes like square cardboard with icing.

"Branding" is something we do to livestock. In fact, the term "brand new" meant something fresh from the fire. Too many marketers and business professionals are trying to "brand" products the same way ranchers brand their cattle: in a way that not only sizzles, but in fact burns.

The problem is that most of these advertisers have a "product"; very few of them actually have a "brand." They just don't know it.

---

* As I mentioned earlier, although this term is overused, I might employ this terminology on occasion throughout this book.

What is a brand?

The dictionary (and by "dictionary" I really mean a webpage I can look up for free and not a heavy bound book I have to dig out of my desk) defines "brand" as "a trademark or distinctive name identifying a product or a manufacturer." Of course, that's the literal way of looking at a brand: it's a name. But a *true brand* is something more. A brand is a product, institution, personality, or service which has developed a clear emotional connection to consumers.

Let's say we're Ed's Vacuum Cleaners*. "We're going to *build our brand*." Ed has been producing high quality vacuum cleaners for fifty years. Ed sells a respectable number of machines each year, both here and abroad. Ed's prices are better than anyone else's. Ed has the best customer service and the longest warranty.

With all due respect to Ed, he doesn't really have a "brand." He has a "product offering." He can sell all the vacuums he wants – out sell Hoover and Dyson combined – but that doesn't make "Ed's" a bona fide brand.

Why? Because there's no real mass emotional connection to the product that Ed is offering. "Ed's" is just another name for a vacuum cleaner. There's no affection, no thrill, no rabid loyalty among Ed's customers for his particular vacuum cleaner. The space is cluttered. Vacuum cleaners are commodity items with little barrier to entry and Ed's Q factor is zero.

Coca-Cola is a brand. Shasta soda is not; it's a product offering. Both are bottled. Both are sold in stores. Both make me burp and taste great with a hot dog. But neither I nor the public at large has a real emotional connection to Shasta. Or to Polar Beverages. Or Acme. Or Ed's. Coca-Cola has an image, an aura, a *je ne sais quoi* that the other products don't have. It's the emotional connection to Coca-Cola (or Pepsi Cola, for that matter) that goes beyond the consumption of sweet fizzy liquid. Years of advertising, messages, merchandising, in-store displays, outdoor signage, and billions of dollars of promotion connects us to specific emotional expressions of the product. Family, friendships,

---

* Not a real vacuum cleaner brand. If someone comes to your door trying to sell you an Ed's vacuum, do NOT invite them in for a demonstration.

sports – and yes – even children and puppies define Coke and Pepsi. That's what makes them brands.

The problem is, how do you get there?

White smoke

Brands can't be anointed; they must be elected. Just like the way Cardinals select a Pope. There is a mysterious process which takes place deep in the conclave of your mind as you evaluate products and incorporate them into your life. Then one day – *poof* – there's white smoke pouring out of your ears and you're saying Novenas about a new hybrid car that you must have!

Although brand names usually sell very well, being a brand has little to do with product preference. Neither does it have to do with being the best sold product in a particular category. Some of my favorite products would not be considered brands, just like not every one of my favorite musicians are considered superstars. There are some microbrews I like that you probably never heard of. I love the HDTV I bought manufactured by Bang & Olufsen[*]. I can't get enough of the Arnold's Multi-grain Sandwich Thins. They make a great sandwich and they only have 100 calories, but Sandwich Thins are no Wonder Bread. And Wonder Bread is a true brand.

A brand is something the consumer must yearn and learn to ask for. They recognize the brand as something *more* than just the sum of the product[†]. It's something which through promotion, advertising, merchandising, and relevance to an ever-emerging market can develop a life of its own. It's something with a fan base. It's something that's revered by users and recognized by non-users. Brands become pop culture icons. None of these things have to do with sales numbers or profit. There are no business metrics to measure what becomes a brand. That's because all the ingredients that fuel these flames are completely and entirely *emotional*.

---

[*] I know, Bang & Olufsen! Who the hell are they? It sounds like a Norwegian marching band.

[†] That may be a mix of addition and multiplication metaphors. I *told* you I was never good at math.

Who makes the cut?

We can have arguments about which product offerings are *true brands*. It would be just like arguing about which ball players belong on the All-Star team or in the Baseball Hall of Fame* and which don't measure up. Or walking through a museum and picking which paintings should be hung alongside the Old Masters. Or scrolling through *Am I Hot or Not.com* and clicking on that blonde[†].

In popular culture and consumer products, there are plenty of examples of offerings that achieve brand status and the also-rans who don't have the same recognition. Here are some:

BRAND	PRODUCT OFFERING
Google	Bing
Hershey	Wilbur Chocolate
McDonald's	Arby's
iPod	Zune
Kleenex	Puffs
Campbell's Soup	Shecky's Matzo Ball Noodle Soup
Walmart	Ma's Convenience Store & Gas Mart
Starbucks	Coffee shop from "Seinfeld"
Red Sox Nation	New England Revolution
The United States	Estonia
Betty	Veronica

Clearly, not every product, no matter how great it may be, grows up to be a true brand. It's not about winning the war over the competition (both McDonald's and Burger King are true brands), but becoming something more than just another commodity to your customers.

At the end of the day, there are a lot more "products" than there are "brands."

---

* Come on! For God's sake admit Pete Rose already!

† You know the one I'm talking about. Cheryl? Yeah, that's right.

Bring it on

Building a brand without a product is like building a house without a foundation. You have to be a legitimate product with significant distribution within a retail channel or channels, packaged right, priced right, and relevant. Then, and only then, can you start working on an emotional connection to that brand through advertising which might result in commanding a presence or awareness.

The misconception that both business and advertisers have been laboring under for years is that it's the ad man's job to "build the brand." That's way easier said than done. It takes massive amounts of money to get the consuming public's attention. One must be extraordinarily clever. Or – you have to have such a unique product that's positioned in such a unique way, or such a niche product that it produces those raving fans. Think of "The Chia Pet" or "The Snuggie*."

It's much easier to take stewardship of a brand (e.g. Coca-Cola has had lots of different advertising agencies throughout the years, including ours). You can reposition a brand; you can make it more relevant or you can inject it with more energy. An organic brand starting from nothing with nominal means will have a very hard time punching through the clutter of today's competitive consumer marketplace.

Some advertisers should settle for a decent product and a profit at year's end and forget about aspiring to the sanctity of brand-hood. It simply won't happen. Or – and here's an amazing idea – create a product offering so different, so consistently good, that consumers will view it as worth telling all their friends about, thereby (dare I say) nearly eliminating the cost of advertising – save the sign on the door.

The cult following

Consumers can move up a brand. In fact, it's always the consumer that makes a product offering become a brand. Sometimes this is done

---

*   Or don't think of the Snuggie. Personally I'm trying to forget it. It's just a backwards bathrobe, people! More like a comfortable straight jacket. I know I mentioned the Snuggie earlier in chapter four, but for me it's deeply rooted and somewhat troubling.

without the assistance of multi-million dollar advertising campaigns or years of steady growth in an industry. Sometimes there's a groundswell of support for an otherwise-unknown product. We say that product has achieved a "cult following."

Everyone knows about the 20 year old housewife from Palo Alto, California who started selling her homemade chocolate chip cookies at the market and turned that into a worldwide venture. But how did Debbi Fields (aka Mrs. Fields) first convince people in 1977 to pay for her cookies? Free samples! After tasting the warm, soft, chewy creations, people started buying en masse. The samplers turned into customers, who then turned into raving fans who drove more business to her single little store. Within five years, the company sold $30 million in cookies at seventy stores from New York City to Honolulu. At its peak, Mrs. Fields Original Cookies Inc. had more than 1,200 stores[*] (today, far fewer brick-and-mortar retail stores – but just check out mrsfields.com).

Sometimes a product with a limited distribution sees the demand increase even more. Consider the historic toy store throw-downs over boxes of Cabbage Patch Kids and Tickle-Me Elmos. Many a parent had an eye gouged or a tooth kicked out trying to get one for Christmas.

For many years in the East, no one could get Coors beer. It wasn't sold anywhere west of the Rockies because it wasn't pasteurized and had to be shipped cold. New Englanders who went skiing in Colorado had to smuggle back six-packs of Coors like they were Cuban cigars[†]. There was a time when pulling a Coors from your fridge and giving it to a friend was something of a status symbol; it was an event. Thus, Coors beer took on a mythical status for the people who just couldn't get it. We always want what we cannot have – it's human nature.

The one thing all these "cult" brands have in common is they were embraced by consumers who valued their product and who would evangelize on their behalves even without advertising. They're labeled as "cult" by the Madison Avenue boys because the products have a small

---

[*] True story: When opening a store in a new mall, Mrs. Field's Original Cookies would design into its stores an external vent which would blow the aroma of fresh-baked cookies into the shopping area as part of their store specs. Talk about appetite appeal!

[†] I've had Cuban cigars. You're not missing anything. They all smell like feet because they're always smuggled into the US in people's socks or sneakers.

but devoted following. I don't know why they sneer at cult products, because Madison Avenue has been trying – and failing – to accomplish the same thing for years (and wasting plenty of money in the process).

Latté trouble

Sometimes branding can backfire and bite you in the ass. If something bad happens that people associate with your brand, it can be awfully hard to change perception and restore your good standing. In fact, you can remain captive to a brand, in which the negative impact of your brand outweighs the positive. For years, American made cars suffered from a reputation of shoddy workmanship. When the Rainman said, "K-Mart sucks," we all knew what he was talking about. And no musician wants to hear that Pat Boone is going to do a cover version of their song.

A good example of a brand name which became an albatross is Philip Morris. Even though the company's product portfolio included Oscar Mayer hotdogs, Maxwell House coffee, and Kraft macaroni & cheese, most people associated Philip Morris with one thing: tobacco. The maker of Marlboro, Virginia Slims, and Parliament cigarettes felt the public backlash against their industry grow steadily over a number of decades. The name "Philip Morris" became inextricably associated with smoking and cancer, no matter how many containers of Kool-Aid or Jell-O they sold. In 2003, Philip Morris Companies Inc. changed its name to Altria Group. What's "altria'" mean? Nobody knows – and that's the point. Out with Philip Morris, in with a name nobody associates with cancer.

Starbucks was a victim of its own branding success. What did the brand "Starbucks" stand for? It was fine coffee served with funny names, the Seattle culture, the hipster Wi-Fi café *feng shui*, and it quickly became a status symbol. They sold it for $3.65 a cup at one airport I recently flew through. When you walked around town with your chai creme half-caf quad Frappuccino ordered "affogato" style[†] in a highly

---

[*] From *altus* or *altior*, the Latin word for "high" – which is what most of the marketing department at Philip Morris must have been when they picked a screwed up name like "Altria."

[†] As in, "*Affogato* buy my coffee for $1.25 at the doughnut shop across the

stylized paper cup with a cardboard sleeve – which used precious natural resources to proclaim Starbucks was saving a rainforest somewhere[*] - it *meant* something. It meant you – the consumer – loved high-priced high-calorie java with names that sound like Italian parrots speaking French. The problem for Starbucks was they began to over-distribute the brand, thereby diluting its specialness. Starbucks cafés were popping up everywhere: in malls, in airports, in bus terminals, inside other larger Starbucks. Who would have thought a successful business model would include putting a second store across the street from your first so people on the opposite sidewalk won't have to cross at the light? [See also, *Manhattan*.]

Once the economy melted, so did Starbucks' cache. A coffee from Starbucks suddenly became a commodity, a luxury that smart consumers couldn't afford and no longer placed a premium on. Yet those expensive retail leases were fixed and profits cooled faster than a forgotten *venti* latté, while at the same time Dunkin Donuts and McDonald's swooped in to market themselves as alternatives to the high-priced cup of joe that Starbucks turned millions of people on to. If you haven't noticed everyone's coffee beans are hand grown, hand selected, and painstakingly brewed to a level that would make Juan Valdez envious!

I love the Starbucks brand. I like the taste of their product and the way they market themselves. In the last two years in response to the economy, the chain has closed a number of low-performing stores thereby reducing overhead and dilution of the brand. Starbucks has also done a great job with their online loyalty programs and re-emphasis on the quality experience of their products. Starbucks, however, must bear responsibility for the recent introduction of its Starbucks Via instant coffee. Really bad, really dumb. It tastes like Sanka.

Is it scalable?

For the most part, the examples of "true brands" I've given have all been major names, products found in every household made by

---

street."

[*]   Apparently, cardboard doesn't come from rainforests. (and yes it was recycled cardboard)

companies with millions — even billions — of dollars in assets and ad budgets. There are some businesses that don't aspire to world-dominance. Can you be a Mom-and-Pop store and still be a true brand*?

The process of becoming a brand is definitely scalable. Whether you're a car dealer, a shopping mall, or a machine shop, you can become a brand by making raving fans out of your customers and clients, no matter your size. Most local products and services achieve brand status by knowing who they are, institutionalizing a culture among their staff, and effectively exporting that culture through their product offering or service on a consistent basis.

In the community in which you live, there are "restaurants" and there are "good places to eat." Everybody knows what the choice establishments for a nice dinner are. They're the places where your friends go and can't wait to tell you about the wonderful meals they had. "Get the salmon," they say. "Save room for dessert." They're our favorites, our old stand-bys. Those restaurants stand above the competition in our minds because we have some emotional connection to them[†].

Local establishments don't have the multi-million dollar budgets that Procter & Gamble or Taco Bell have, but in some ways they're at an advantage when it comes to starting a genuine grassroots dialogue with customers. In small to medium sized businesses, the employees are usually not perceived by customers as nameless, faceless drones working for "The Man[‡]." The owner of the establishment can meet and greet the customers personally. Becoming an online fan of a local boutique seems more organic, more genuine than clicking onto an overly-slick, corporate website for The Gap. It's easier for the little guys to come off as real and seem more accessible to the consumer because *they are*! You're more likely to take stock in an email that came from the general manager of the local Jeep dealership than an email that was "written" to you by the president of Chrysler.

For example, a small bridal shop can cultivate raving fans with good customer service and an active presence on the web. Fewer wives-to-be

---

[*] This is a rhetorical question. The answer is yes. If you stopped to think about the answer to that question, you're probably reading at a third-grade level.

[†] The good times you had there, Aunt Mabel's 80th birthday fete, a bachelor party which may have involved police intervention.

[‡] Larry.

are picking up the $5.99 bridal magazines to shop for wedding dresses and more are shopping online. Once they find a designer or dress style they like, they search for a local boutique in which to try it on. Using search engine optimization (the process of employing HTML code techniques that make a website appear closer to the top of the list when search engines display results) the bridal store can catch the attention of customers interested in their lines. By deploying social media tools brides can ask questions of sales associates or post photos from their wedding. If the bride likes her experience, she may tweet about it or post a link on Facebook. Now instead of anticipating future sales among just the bridesmaids in her party, the bride will endorse the shop to her whole network: *all* of her friends and family. Regardless of the network member's age or gender, they'll likely keep that store in mind when asked about where someone can get a good wedding dress.

Today more than ever brand status is achieved by creating raving fans who will share their experiences about a product or service with the other consumers in their networks.

Sweet Baby Ray's gourmet barbecue sauce is a client of ours. Their slogan is "The Sauce is the Boss!" and they really know what they're talking about. It helps that Sweet Baby Ray's is an excellent product (don't tell the account manager, but it practically sells itself), so cultivating raving fans across the country has come naturally for the brand. When we conducted a social media audit for the company, we were surprised at how many Sweet Baby Ray's customers were making homemade videos extolling the brand and posting these testimonials on YouTube. Most were doing their own "commercials" endorsing SBR and offering cooking tips. Some were doing really wacky things, like drinking it from the bottle or, in one bizarre case, actually pouring the stuff on one of their kids. The toddler didn't seem to mind and he laughed as Daddy licked it off his fingers and smacked his lips. These were people who were making their own heartfelt (if not always tasty or tasteful) pitches for this brand. They evangelized for Sweet Baby Ray's, gave testimonials, all of them unsolicited. Now *those* are some raving fans!

Watchu doin wit that cattle prod?

Why are consumers so interested in "brands"? Because the brand preferences we choose make a statement about who we are. The kind of car you drive is often a status symbol in our society. The same for the clothing designers and even the jeans you wear. Or the brand of beer or wine you enjoy at a bar. People make an assumption about you if you're drinking a bottle of Heineken or if you pull out a can of Pabst Blue Ribbon (now making a resurgence with younger price-sensitive drinkers under the acronym PBR). What kind of person must you be if you ask the bartender for Grey Goose vodka or for Jack Daniels? (These brands have become so well established that they are ordered in bars around the world in secret code: "Give me a Jack and Coke," or "I'll have a Goose and tonic with lime.")

The brands we select validate us as consumers. We like to show off our new Nikon digital SLR cameras and crow about the latest iteration of our Blackberry Curve. Why buy a Rolex when you can have a Timex? Because for a person of your status, only the Rolex will do[*].

For those people who eschew brand names, their choice of non-capitulation says something about them too. It says they don't worry about tags, labels, or status. ("Look at me! I don't need no stinkin' designer coffee from Starbucks!") It says they're more concerned with the price and practicality of items than the perceived value of those items. While others walk to work sipping from cups that read "Starbucks" or "Dunkin Donuts," they're content to drink coffee in a plain white Styrofoam cup that probably came from a bus station vending machine. No bottled water for these non-conformists. Their maverick status is a thing of pride.

And why not? The term "maverick" comes from the Old West. Rancher Samuel Maverick's claim to fame was that – unlike all of his contemporaries – his cattle were *not* branded.

---

[*] Besides, Roger Federer wears and pitches Rolex, and he's a pretty cool dude.

Chapter ten

Get Them Out of Here, They're Celebrities

Fighting with ball players, politicians, impressionists, and vampires

One of the biggest falsehoods of advertising is that a celebrity endorsement can sell any product. It's a hard impression to break because, in part, commercials with celebrities tend to be more memorable. Jackie Gleason sold Nescafé in the 1950s. Joe DiMaggio sold Mr. Coffee in the 1970s. Rachel Ray sold Dunkin Donuts coffee in the 2000s. Santa Claus sold Coca-Cola in the 1930s. Michael Jackson sold Pepsi in the 1980s. Bo knows football and baseball, but Bo "don't know Diddley" for Nike. People remember those commercials, but not everyone who watched them was convinced by the celebrity to purchase the product.

There was a period in the 1980s, right after the rock 'n' roll cola wars, in which celebrities would only do commercial product endorsements in Japan. Western stars were huge in the Far East, but many actors and their agents feared they'd look like sell-outs to American audiences. Today, it's professionally and culturally acceptable again for famous people to appear in commercials. But many of these campaigns are off-target – or worse – a waste of money because the connection between the celeb and the product is often quite unclear to the customer.

Derek Jeter appears in advertisements for Gatorade. The association is clear: a world-class athlete uses this product to hydrate. For the discerning amateur athlete the idea of using a product that's "good enough" for Jeter may be appealing*. Gatorade is leveraging Jeter's athletic talent, not just his celebrity.

---

* This is different than an advertiser trying to imply that the Gatorade supplies the

PAY NO ATTENTION TO THAT MAN BEHIND THE CURTAIN

Peyton Manning appears in advertisements for…well…just about *everything*. DirecTV, Sprint, Oreos…Manning will stand on a corner with a sandwich board for $100 if you ask him. The quarterback's problem is not that he's over-exposed – although he is. The problem is the products he's hawking have little to do with Peyton Manning – and some of these consumers (amazingly) don't even know who the great quarterback is!

I'll admit I like the MasterCard commercials in which he blithely plays the "priceless" idiot savant. Even the Sprint ad in which he's wearing the horribly fake wig and mustache weakly pretending to be anyone other than Peyton Manning is funny*. But neither of these products really have much to do with an NFL player (I mean, are you *surprised* that a rich athlete uses a credit card?). What are the *bona fides* that give Manning credible license to dispense advice about Sony HDTVs? Or web-enabled cell phones? Even the advertiser who could likely get the most out of an association with Manning, Reebok, punted their 30 seconds by airing an ad showing Peyton, Eli, and Archie Manning making breakfast. "You got the pancakes, I got the eggs," he barks in a huddle. "On one. Ready. Break!"

For every celebrity campaign that seems made in heaven (Michael Jordan and Nike) there are dozens of others that make you want to scratch your head (Mikhail Gorbachev for Pizza Hut? Kathy Lee Gifford for Carnival Cruises? Regis and Kelly for TD Bank? Phil Ruzzito for the Money Store? "Holy cow- it's a hit!"). And celebrities have career paths of their own that sometimes leave their advertiser regretting their association (EA Sports, Powerade, and Hasbro all drop kicked Michael Vick; Kobe Bryant fouled out with McDonald's and Nutella; and Michael Phelps blew it with Frosted Flakes). Fame is fleeting and every star is one Late Show staffer away from being blackmailed or blackballed.

---

athlete with his greatness. Mel Allen, for example, would follow a Mickey Mantle home run by exclaiming the Yankee had "eaten his Wheaties" that day. Today, your advertising gland would excrete all over a ploy like that.

* Funny is good. If an advertiser uses a celebrity to make the joke, that's their prerogative. But any union actor can give a punch line; not every actor can hit a WR on a slant route in the red zone.

Celebrity endorsements aren't always successful. Tiger Woods, for example, took $15 million from GM, but his ads didn't help Buick sales. And that was *before* he drove his Escalade into a tree and a dozen mistresses fell out (along with his endorsements for TAG Heuer, Gillette, AT&T, *et al*). But tapping into the right attribute of the right star for the right product can lead to good results.

So now having indicated my general disdain for the use of celebrities as spokesmen let me share a few of the ones I worked with. Each proved successful – but not all were easy and some, in hindsight, I wish we might have passed on.

Champagne wishes and caviar dreams

In the mid 1980s, the states of New Hampshire, Vermont, and Maine embarked on an endeavor to form a consortium to sell online lottery tickets within all three states. The idea of combining the markets to create otherwise-unattainable big jackpots by creating a larger player base would become the Tri-State Lottery Commission, the nation's first multi-state lottery. Today, multi-state initiatives like Powerball and Mega-Millions are commonplace (as are jackpots that grow into the $200 and $300 million range). But in 1986, the idea of winning $10 or $15 million on a lottery ticket in Northern New England was heady, fantastic, and still viewed as a novel experience.

Coordinating the marketing priorities and visions of three separate lottery staffs (not to mention three separate lottery commissions, governors, and legislatures) was a tricky business. After some power-sharing experimentation, the ad agencies for the states formed a limited partnership, "Pick Three LTD," a creative coalition that would steward advertising for the new lottery. My firm worked with Jim Hormel of Communicators Group in Brattleboro, Vermont and with David Body of Body & Company of Portland, Maine.

At the same time the new Tri-State Megabucks game was about to roll out, "Lifestyles of the Rich and Famous" was enjoying a spectacular run on syndicated television, fueling a new era of über-celebrity worship. The show featured host Robin Leach* sipping bubbly and nibbling

---

* A terribly unfortunate last name for a man who did the kind of suck-up journalism required of him.

beluga with movie stars and captains of industry who flaunted their avarice for the cameras. Viewers were drawn to the voyeuristic show because, in the host's words, we all had "champagne wishes and caviar dreams."

State lotteries – whatever you may feel about them – are not about good financial investments. Everybody knows the odds are long and the lotteries don't purport otherwise. Like beer and cigarettes and french fry consumption, the industry stresses responsible use of their product. What you get when you buy a lottery ticket is not a promise of a financial return – it is a license to dream. That small paper ticket in your pocket gives you license to dream right up until that next big drawing. With apologies to Shakespeare, it's not the play but *the dream's the thing*. That said, it seemed to us that Robin Leach would be a great spokesman for the dream concept behind the advertising campaign for the Tri-State Lottery.

Biggest thing since the hula hoop

The theme of the campaign was "Just Imagine." Robin Leach could not have been a better person to work with. The commercial campaign was shot over a series of days on a small sound stage in a less-than inviting block in New York's Hell's Kitchen. Robin was always early to the set, chipper, and ready to go. He took direction graciously and eagerly. He never complained about a script or how many takes were required to get it right.

After a day of shooting stand-ups of our spokesman imploring players to "just imagine the possibilities," the other members of the Pick Three Team and I began talking about where in Manhattan we might eat that night. We hailed from Northern New England, but Robin worked to impress us as if we were from Madison Avenue.

"Gentlemen, gentlemen," Robin said in his famously sonorous English accent, "I know just the place you should go! It's my favorite establishment in New York! The chef is a prodigy and the food is brilliant! I'll have my assistant phone ahead!"

That evening when Jim, David, and I sauntered into a packed East Side eatery we were greeted by a bustling bar crowd and lots of New Yorkers (many dressed in dark suits – which had me worried that I might run into some of the same Dunkin Donuts agency guys I had pissed off years earlier). When we strolled into the restaurant there was a large table in the best part of the establishment ready for us. We were pampered by tuxedoed waiters. We felt like stars ourselves. At one point a huge chilled bottle of Dom Pérignon arrived at our table. "Complements of Mr. Leach," the waiter said. He then motioned to a corner table where Robin Leach himself, a pair of wannabe starlets on each arm, raised his own glass of Champagne and saluted us. Surely the gesture was taken from chapter one of the "How to Suck Up and Influence People" playbook, but from Robin it seemed both fitting and sincere. He paid for the champagne; we paid for our own dinner.

The ad campaign was very effective. Using scripts that mimicked the "Lifestyles" show, writing lines in the spokesman's unique voice, Robin was featured in 15 television and radio commercials imploring people to "buy a ticket and just imagine!" Sales for the new Megabucks tickets were strong and the Lifestyles of the Rich and Famous homage reinforced the image of the Tri-State Lottery as dream-maker.

Robin was such a pleasant professional to work with that we hired him again to work with another one of our clients, Contel Systems. We flew him to Hawaii for a Contel sales convention with a "Lifestyles" theme. For months leading up to the event, the husbands or wives of leading salespeople were getting phone messages voiced by Leach on their home answering machines. Today, we would term these "robo-calls" in politics. "Make sure your spouse makes their numbers because I want to see *you* in Kauai!" The telephone and coordinated direct mail campaign was a huge success. More than 250 Contel sales reps qualified for the trip to Hawaii. The first night of the convention Robin and the Contel CEO arrived in a white Rolls Royce to a lavish welcome party held under a white tent on a sprawling sugar cane plantation. Everything was deliciously over-the-top and the conference-goers loved it. The client was happy. Robin was happy. We were happy.

The night we arrived in Hawaii just before the conference began several colleagues from the agency and I took Robin to dinner at the Weston Kauai Resort. At one point during dinner conversation turned to Robin's success and the quirky personality he had parlayed into a unique brand of celebrity. "Robin, don't you ever get tired of all this?" someone asked. For the right price any celebrity will give a testimonial;

few of them ever do so as enthusiastically as Robin Leach. "I take every minute I can get," he said, "because I am nothing more than a contemporary version of the hula-hoop! I'm the biggest flash-in-the-pan you've ever seen and I'm going to make as much as I can, as long as I can, because retirement is lonely, cold, and there ain't a lot to be done once I've run my course."

I was amazed at his candor. He *got it* and Robin Leach was one of the very few celebrities I have worked with who clearly did not take himself too seriously. But most of all, he delivered the goods as a true professional. In my experience his kind of celebrity turned out to be the exception, *not* the rule.

The impression that I get

Another Tri-State Megabucks campaign we created a few years later carried the tag line, "What Would You Do If You Were Rich?" To go with the new tagline was a new spokesman: impressionist Rich Little. The concept was a series of commercials with lines to camera from actual lottery players describing what they would do with their Megabucks winnings intercut with clips of Little made up to look like (and sound like) various celebrities.

Much like the Robin Leach campaigns, a year's worth of commercials would be shot over a couple of days on a sound stage, this time in Boston at a large studio in Everett then known as High Output. The morning of the first day of the shoot I was to meet Rich Little in Boston's Back Bay in the Bristol Lounge at The Four Seasons Hotel, where we had agreed to put him up for the week. Out of nowhere, a bald man in a plaid jacket grabbed my hand and began pumping it.

"Hey Pat, nice to meet you! Mel Bishop here." Mel quickly told me his life story and made me aware of the fact that he'd been "in the business" for nearly 40 years and that he had worked with stars of every caliber from "the Catskills to Broadway, to Vegas and beyond!" He was like a Mel Brooks character – part Max Bialystock, part vaudeville veteran – but he couldn't have been a nicer guy. Mel was Rich's Road Manager and traveled with him ensuring things went smoothly. I knew Mel would be there from our negotiations with Rich's agents. If Rich Little was travelling to Boston to shoot lottery ads, Mel had to be there. At the time I wasn't sure why Mel was such a necessity. I came to understand once I saw the glum face of Mr. Little, looking very much like he had just swallowed a lemon.

"There's a rip in my carpet," he grunted. Sitting at a table, his arms folded, was an irascible Rich Little. I wasn't sure I heard him correctly, so I asked him to repeat himself. "There's a rip in my carpet. There's a stain on my couch. This place is a dump," he deadpanned.

I waited for a punch line. I assumed he was joking. He wasn't.

Flabbergasted that anyone would find Boston's finest hotel "a dump," I said I'd go see what I could do. Mel pulled me aside and, in his showbizzy Catskills accent, attempted to translate for his client.

"What I think Rich means is he'd like a room that's a little nicer, a little fresher." He gave me a wink. "Maybe something with a better view. Some flowers…"

"…That's not what I'm saying!" Rich groused from across the room. "This place is a dump…"

I went to the front desk to attempt to procure a different suite for Mr. Little, and I realized my experience on this project was going to be very different than our previous lottery work with Robin Leach.

Who wouldn't want to be Rich?

In order to achieve the effect we wanted, we brought in a special make-up artist from Hollywood to apply prosthetics, wigs, and custom make-up to make Rich look just like the people he was impersonating. The scripts called for Rich to play over a dozen iconic characters, from Johnny Carson to Jack Benny to Richard Nixon, Arnold Schwarzenegger or the Godfather. It seemed to me the one character he had the most trouble playing on camera was himself.

Much like a feature film, none of the spots – or even the tag lines – were going to be shot in order. Director Sean Tracy decided to shoot the ending taglines first. This required Rich Little to play himself instead of a character. An off camera voiceover would introduce him saying, "Here's Rich Little for Tri-State Megabucks." We'd then cut to Rich as himself wearing a blue blazer seated against a seamless background. He'd read a simple line to the camera from the teleprompter: "What would you do if you were rich?" "Who wouldn't want to be rich?" "Wouldn't it be fantastic to be rich?" Pretty straight forward, right?

"I don't get this," Rich hollered across the set in mid take. "What does this even mean? Why am I doing this?"

"Cut!" yelled an assistant director.

It was like he didn't *get it*.

I knew part of his agreement required his creative approval of final scripts, which were sent to him weeks before we started filming. We had never received any feedback from him or his management. They were simple lines, but he struggled doing them. Perhaps he couldn't see the play on words (Rich/rich?). Or that because he couldn't read the line as a character – say Jimmy Stewart, Ronald Reagan, or George Bush – he couldn't see how this straight intro fit into the overall commercial concept. I found this hard to fathom. It was clear to me he had not read the scripts. So now, he was making everyone miserable.

It wasn't until later in the day, when he came out dressed as George Burns or Arnold Schwarzenegger, that Rich Little seemed to come alive. It took hours to do the make-up and wardrobe and lighting before he even got in front of the camera. Then it took a while for him to get warmed up (while very expensive 35 mm film stock was rolling through the camera gate). Eventually, he'd catch fire and the performer we all remembered from "The Tonight Show" would emerge. That's when he could truly perform. He'd go off-script, riffing as these characters just like he did in his Vegas act, and getting laughs from the whole crew. But the impressionist never seemed to capture the same energy or enthusiasm for the scripted lines he was being paid for. He liked his own material better than ours.

Contemplating another complex costume change the make-up artist said, "We're going to have to wash his hair." "Don't wash my hair!" the man impersonating Andy Rooney screamed. "Rich is sensitive about his hair," Mel interjected. "Rich doesn't want people touching his hair." I wondered how much more bizarre this thing could get. Somehow the make-up and styling people worked this all out and an hour later Rich emerged on the set as someone else entirely.

The sad part about all of this was that he was an incredibly talented guy and when he got going the copy worked just as we'd intended it.

The stuff was great. I knew when we intercut Rich's impressions with real winners they would kill!

The next morning back at The Four Seasons, Mel pulled me aside. There was another problem with Rich's room. He didn't like the color of the walls or some damn thing, so we moved him to yet another suite. By the time the week was over we had moved Rich to four different rooms, none of which seemed to meet his expectations.

The "What Would You Do If You Were Rich" campaign was also considered a success by any measure. For the investment of $45,000 (Rich Little's fee divided among the three states), Tri-State Megabucks did over $100 million in sales that year. The ads also won all sorts of industry awards for excellence. The campaign worked because it leveraged Rich's talents and juxtaposed them with testimonials from real people who played and in some cases had actually won the lottery. We were able to use photos of Rich as these iconic characters in print ads and in point of sale material. For me, the best part of the campaign was that the shoot was over! I was headed back to New Hampshire and Rich was headed back to Las Vegas, Mel Bishop in tow. I've stayed at The Four Seasons in Boston many times since the shoot and never found a stain in the carpet.

...It has to be good

One celebrity we used that really fit the bill for a client's campaign was the late character actor Mason Adams. Fans of the show "Lou Grant" will remember him as newspaper editor Charlie Hume[*]; however, Mason's claim to fame was not his face, but his voice. Mason Adams was the voiceover for TV commercials such as Crest toothpaste ("Helps stop cavities *before* they start") and Cadbury Crème Eggs ("No-bunny knows Easter better than him"). But the pitch-perfect tagline that will always be replayed in his dulcet tones is that of Smucker's preserves. As you read this next sentence, there's no way your brain will not process

---

[*] Please don't confuse Mr. Adams with Daryl Anderson, the actor who played Dennis "Animal" Price. "Animal" was the photographer with the 70s hippie 'fro, beard and coke-bottle glasses. Anderson, while certainly a fine actor, did little after "Lou Grant" except for five appearances on "$10,000 Pyramid" against Susan Richardson of "Eight is Enough."

it so you hear it in Mason Adams' classic voice: "With a name like Smucker's, it has to be good."

We were doing advertising for HealthSource, an HMO that was revolutionizing the way health insurance was offered to employers and their staffs. They were among the first health maintenance organizations here in the East, before the days when the letters "HMO" became regarded by some consumers as greedy, trendy, and in some cases, offering poor coverage. HealthSource was breaking new ground. They were going to reward people for going to the gym or quitting smoking. They were going to keep costs low by working with a selected network of primary care doctors. They were building physician networks to increase referrals through their contracted physicians and providers. Their focus was going to be keeping people healthy, not just paying the bills when they got sick.

Marketing a product like health insurance is difficult because it's a commodity that a consumer accesses usually through their employer, but doesn't select on their own. Usually the company health plans are picked by human resource managers whose criteria for choosing may not always match that of the beneficiaries. Part of our strategy was to create awareness and demand for HealthSource among employees, and encourage them to ask their HR departments for the HealthSource option. But key to this strategy was building confidence among consumers about this little-known product and the reliable benefits of HealthSource coverage.

Mason had a warm, distinguished, folksy voice that oozed gentle gravitas. It was a recognizable voice. When Mason read the scripts for HealthSource, it made people feel comforted and comfortable with the product. Remember, back in the early 1990s, the HMO model was still viewed by many consumers as new and a little unsettling. The voice people knew and recognized as the purveyor of Smucker's was the perfect choice to make customers feel secure and comfortable with their insurance coverage.

Unlike using Derek Jeter to sell Gatorade – in which a professional athlete is promoting a product that benefits other athletes – Mason Adams wasn't associated with medical care or insurance*. He didn't dress in a lab coat; in his tweed jacket and tie he looked more like

---

* He's not a doctor and unfortunately he never played one on TV.

the Head Master at a prestigious New England boarding school. The celebrity attribute that we leveraged was his credibility. Using a voice as recognizable as Mason Adams' alerted viewers the HealthSource product was a major league player, a legitimate contender with the likes of major national indemnity insurers. Also, people associated his voice with sincerity, safety, and soundness. Mason created a halo of trust around the HealthSource product that a fast-talking car salesman or athlete simply could not.

Mason was hardly a *prima donna* on the set. He was gracious and accommodating, and he loved to do the work. As a favor to me, I asked him if he'd record the greeting for my home answering machine. He good-naturedly obliged and one day while recording radio copy in the studio he improvised: "Leave a message and they'll get back to you. Because with a name like 'Griffin,' they have to be good."

Mason Adams sold a lot of insurance plans for HealthSource and was a true gentleman to work with. I will remember the years we worked with him fondly. More importantly, the significant increase he helped the company achieve in its enrollment, retention, and long-term market position.

Go long

The New Hampshire Lottery stayed away from celebrity spokesmen for a few years until we launched a campaign in the mid 1990s with comedian/actor Jerry Van Dyke. The younger brother of Dick Van Dyke, Jerry's earlier claim to fame was having turned down the role of Gilligan on "Gilligan's Island" in 1964 and later taking the lead in the epochal bomb "My Mother the Car" in 1965. Jerry's career was resurrected in 1989 as Luther Van Dam on ABC's "Coach," for which he received four consecutive Emmy nominations for best supporting actor.

Jerry had spent many years as a stand-up comedian, so he kept his own counsel about what material was, in his opinion, "funny." "I know what's funny," he'd say to us on the set. "Five is not a funny number. Seven! Now that's a funny number! I'm going to say 'seven.'" Even if we'd point out he needed to say 'five' because the copy in the spot was promoting a $5.00 instant scratch ticket, he'd still insist on saying 'seven.'

Because he felt he knew what was funny, Jerry liked to change up the script, often improvising copy or punch lines. This is sometimes a good thing as I've pointed out, as the comedic sense of timing and writing is often part of what you're paying for when you lure a comedian/celebrity to do your commercials. But this was dangerous water to get into with ad copy for a state government agency that had to be blessed by the client and carefully vetted. "How about we do it this way?" he'd offer. In the spirit of artistic compromise, we'd say, "Sure. Read it once like we have it in the script and once the way you'd like to do it." Now with something invested in making his version the best, Jerry would occasionally mumble or give a half-assed performance of the original line before exploding with energy and zeal for his own interpretation (actors! – never trust 'em!).

In one spot Jerry appeared with a chimpanzee. "I've worked with monkeys before," Jerry proclaimed. "I know what I'm doing." The animal's trainer looked on aghast as Jerry began to berate the chimp*. "I have to establish that I'm the alpha male if I'm going to have a relationship with this monkey," he lectured. Needless to say, the chimp didn't take well to Jerry's attempt to show him who was boss. And while we eventually got a great spot out of the effort, I remember telling copy writer Sean Bice that he should forget any future creative concept which involved monkeys.

Please note as well the chimp was never in any danger of physical or emotional harm on the set with Jerry – which is more than I can say for myself.

The vampire's bite

Despite the fact that he was not easy to work with, Jerry Van Dyke was a wonderful man and was a very likable lottery spokesman. When we met for the first time in the early 1990s, the creative team and I took Jerry and his wife to Legal Sea Foods in Boston the night before we began the first day of shooting. When other diners spotted

---

* These were in the days before we saw news stories about domesticated chimpanzees on anti-anxiety medicines attacking their Connecticut neighbors.

him they shouted out "Hey, Luther!" his character's name on "Coach." Jerry agreeably waved back, talked enthusiastically with fans, and was willing throughout dinner to sign autographs and pose for pictures with passersby who immediately recognized him. It was over dinner that we learned from his wife Shirley that the Van Dyke's had distantly known OJ and Nicole Brown Simpson. This was not long after the OJ Simpson trial and all of us were mesmerized by Shirley's passionate recalling of the late woman's life with OJ, her amiable personality, and the impression she made on the few occasions they had met. Jerry was ravenous for dinner (although it turns out he hated seafood) and let his wife take command of the story while he devoured a steak. When Shirley had finished describing this life cut tragically short most of us at the table were speechless. Jerry, his comic timing spot on, deadpanned, "I wanna ask one question: if an ex-football player had to murder his wife how come it couldn't have been Frank Gifford?" Needless to say, we all broke up.

    The next day we were shooting a Halloween ticket-themed commercial on a sound stage filled with fog and spooky lighting. Jerry was dressed as a comical vampire, his hair slicked back in a funny do. He was mad about something that day and stormed off the set. "This isn't funny," he decreed. "I want to talk to you," he hissed, pointing at me.

    I followed Jerry into a private room that overlooked the studio. It had a sliding glass door that the star slammed as he began to yell at me. "I don't need to be doing this," he said. "I could be in L.A. right now sitting by a pool or back at home in Arkansas." Realizing I too could be doing other things at that moment, I yelled back at him. He needed to live up to his contract and read the lines he'd been given. We were nose-to-nose, pointing fingers and waving arms. He threatened to quit, I threatened to fire him, and so it went.

    The studio outside us was ensconced in darkness, while the room we had gone into was lit very well with bright florescent lights. I realized that the floor-to-ceiling glass doors – while relatively soundproof – were providing a perfect *tableau vivant* for the entire crew, the cast, the folks from the office, and the clients. Everyone was able to see me and Jerry Van Dyke– dressed like Bela Lugosi – jawing at one another about whether the number eight was funnier than the number four or something like that. I wanted to drive a stake through my *own* heart. Suddenly we realized we were providing entertainment for the stunned on-lookers and agreed we would press on with the copy as written.

For three years, Jerry did a great job for the Lottery and he continued to sell tickets at a record pace.

Isn't it splendid?

My heart breaks to say it, but the worst celebrity I ever dealt with was one of my boyhood idols: Ted Williams. He may have been the greatest hitter who ever lived, but he wasn't afraid to make a pitch either. Over the years he promoted Chesterfield cigarettes, Sears, Moxie, and Nissen bread. I thought working with him would be a breeze. At this point in my career, I should have known better.

Ted was one of the few celebrities I had a personal relationship with before a professional one. My late father-in-law, Sam Tamposi, was a real estate wizard and a limited partner in the Boston Red Sox. In the 1970s, Sam and his long-time partner, Gerald Nash, developed a 20,000 acre tract of land northwest of Tampa called Citrus Hills. Within a few years, what had been watermelon fields and old-growth forest was now the site of 10,000 homes, tennis courts, a massive club house, a pool, and two championship golf courses — all located in one of the most beautiful and unspoiled parts of the Sunshine State. In the 1980s, Sam was able to bring his friend, Ted Williams, into the fold as the spokesman for Citrus Hills.

When Ted Williams would visit New England, he often stayed at my father-in-law's home in Nashua, NH (across the street from where my wife Sally and I were living). He called me "Irish," and wasn't shy about dispensing marital advice to me in front of Sally[*]. During one visit, in which Sam's house was undergoing renovations, Ted Williams stayed with us. It was a thrill for our paperboy who, when word got out, delivered the afternoon paper to the front door in hopes of getting a glimpse of the Splendid Splinter. It wasn't long before every kid in the neighborhood was at the door with balls, gloves, and posters looking for autographs.

---

[*] He referred to her as "The Princess," which was only one of the reasons why I never took his marital advice.

"Goddammit, I'm not going to sign any more crap!" he loudly complained. This was just before dinner and after Ted had a scotch or two under his belt. Ted was famous for being a curmudgeon and a contrarian. He was like a real-life John Wayne character. Big, loud, and never afraid to say what he thought. He was so uninhibited, unfiltered, that he bordered on being anti-social. "I'm not here to be the family house pet. Get rid-a-those kids." Before long, Ted relented and gave every kid an autograph.

On occasion, at my father-in-law's request, it was my job to pick up Ted at Fenway Park and drive him back to Nashua. The drill was for me to pull up to the players' gate at Fenway Park where the Boston cops would let me through and the Hall-of-Famer would be waiting for me[*]. One time I pulled up and Ted was nowhere to be found. "He's still up in the owner's box," the security guy told me. I left my car at the gate and made my way up to Mrs. Jean Yawkey's box. There, Ted Williams was king and he was proudly holding court. He held the late Jean Yawkey (widow of iconic Red Sox owner Tom Yawkey) in great esteem and always enjoyed spending time in her suite. He was surrounded by former players and friends of his from the old days, rapping about fastballs, curve balls, and loose women. He was often loud, profane, and the center of attention: quintessential Ted Williams.

"Whaddya say, Irish?" It was getting into the later innings. We still had to make an exit through the public concourses of Fenway and there was no way he was going to make it out unmolested with the grandstands now beginning to empty out. "Ted, it's time to go," I said patiently.

In order to get the Red Sox's greatest player out of Fenway Park alive, over a dozen ushers, Fenway security guards, and Boston cops had to form a phalanx around Ted and I. "Get going, Irish. Get a move on," he would bellow as he shoved me around inside the center of this security scrum. Once on the concourse, in the bottom of the eighth inning, we had to bulldoze our way through swarms of adoring fans, many of them kids. The people reached out, looking for a hand to shake or a back to pat, just to say they met the great Ted Williams. Cameras

---

[*] Ted would then proceed to tell me how to drive. "Slow down, for Christ's sake. You're right on this guy's ass. Get in this lane. What's the hurry, Irish?" It was always a nightmare.

flashed. Autograph pens were shoved toward Ted. "*No hablo español!*" For some reason Ted either thought all of Boston spoke Spanish or that his fans might believe he didn't speak English. I never really figured it out.

But the fruit is impossible to eat

My professional experience with Ted came in 1988 when I shot a series of commercials for Citrus Hills. Ted lived at Citrus Hills having fled the Florida Keys a few years earlier. He was, of course, the spokesman. I flew to Florida, with a television crew, and brought Ted to different locations that showed off the property. I should have known that he would be a bear to work with*. We traveled from one location to another in a large van that held our star, our crew, and our camera equipment. Ted sat in the front seat where he could sit with his arms folded across his chest, bark instructions to the driver, and generally hold court, all while dispensing his unsolicited thoughts on everything from baseball to politics.

The Splendid Splinter turned around and grilled his fellow passengers about who among them was going to vote for George Bush in the upcoming 1988 Presidential election. I was the only one who raised his hand. "What?" he exploded. "Do you mean the rest of you are for *Dukakis*? What are you, a bunch of fucking *communists*? Michael Dukakis, Jesus Christ!" The crew was nonplussed; they apparently had seen enough of Teddy Ballgame at this point to know to just ignore him and allow Ted to be Ted.

"We have to stop for lunch," I told Ted. He objected, saying the crew could just push through to the next location and finish up early. In any event, *he* wasn't hungry. "I have to feed the crew," I explained to Ted. "I *have* to give them a lunch break." The retired ballplayer called them all a bunch of "pussies," and posed all sorts of rhetorical questions about their character and collective manhood. Nonetheless he argued

---

* If you won't take my word for it, go to www.tedwilliamsblooper.com. Someone, somewhere got a hold of the outtakes from that shoot and posted them on the Internet. In the clip, you'll see a tanned Ted Williams go off on a profane jag because a truck in the distance revved its engine in the middle of a sound take. You can hear my voice off-camera in between his expletives.

for a while and then agreed that a short break was fine, but that no one should take too long or get "too goddamn comfortable."

We pulled into a Burger King in Crystal River where the crew took refuge from the Florida heat inside. Ted got out of the van and walked around the parking lot by himself. "Come on inside," I urged. "It's hot. I'll get you something to drink."

"No. I don't want anything." He was sulking. While the small army that was our "crew" chowed down on Whoppers and fries, the greatest ballplayer in history was moping outside alone in the parking lot, pacing like a caged lion and none too happy about the situation. I finally went inside with the crew to grab something, keeping one eye on my lunch and the other on my steaming spokesman from inside the restaurant.

As Ted continued to pace, I noticed a large conversion van pull into the parking lot. It stopped by Ted just in front of the restaurant entrance. The vehicle was being driven by a couple in their 60s. The husband put the van in park and opened up the side door. Their passenger was a young girl who appeared to have severe disabilities. She was in a wheelchair and didn't seem able to communicate. The van was equipped with some kind of mechanical winch that allowed the couple to get the girl out of the van and back into a waiting wheelchair. Ted was fascinated by the machinations involved in operating the wench and getting the young girl secured in the swing. In fact, he wasn't content just to watch; he had to insert himself in the procedure and give assistance as he saw fit. "More to the right now. Not so fast, not so fast." These orders were firm – but his voice was smaller, gentler…kinder. Ted joined the old man in steadying the child as the hydraulic arm lifted her and placed her gently in the chair. This was not the recalcitrant "John Wayne" Ted I had been dealing with all day.

"She's a beautiful little girl," he declared as I came outside. "How old is she now?" he asked the parents. They indicated the girl who suffered from severe cerebral palsy from birth had just turned 18-years-old. "She's a sweetheart," Ted said, kindly putting one of his big bear paws on the girl's shoulder – gently fixing her dark hair.

The couple – completely unaware of this Samaritan's true identity – wheeled the disabled girl into the restaurant as the satiated camera crew began to slowly return to our van. I approached Ted gently. "That was really something, what you did," I said. He ignored the compliment.

"Did you see what they had to do to get that poor young girl out of that van?" he said, without his characteristic bluster. "The mechanical thing they had to use to move her around? Wasn't that somethin'? Those people...those are the kind of people who are going straight to Heaven. Good people. We need more of them in this world, Irish."

It really touched me. Ted could unquestionably be a bastard when he wanted to, a man with all sorts of complex issues. He was adored for decades by the most demanding baseball fans in the world, yet he refused to tip his cap to them but once. He was foul-mouthed and unapologetic. He could care less if he hurt your feelings and – at least in my experience with him – he could not conceive of an instance when he had ever been mistaken. But deep-down, he clearly had a great big heart. All the legends about Ted Williams' soft spot for sick children, for those Jimmy Fund kids, were all true. Helping that family was a gesture that really humanized him for me, that took away some of the sting of that difficult day as I saw a side of Ted few people ever really did up close. The Splendid Splinter, it turns out under all that bluster, really was a splendid human being.

"Now," Ted said, putting his hands on his hips and turning toward the van in that Florida parking lot, "let's get the hell outta here." The Old Ted was back!

Nice work if you can avoid it

Forever fearful of being upstaged by the cute, the precocious, or the otherwise uncontrollable, WC Fields famously muttered, "Never work with animals or children." I'd have to add one more to the Axis of Evil in the Fields Doctrine: "Never work with animals, children, or celebrities (if possible)."

Especially if one of them thinks it's a good idea to antagonize a chimpanzee.

Chapter eleven

Of Doughnuts, Beer, Soda & Republicans

Politics as product

The date was February 1st, 2000. I had just spent several long months campaigning in New Hampshire with a man I thought should be the next President of the United States. That night, the attention of the world was on our tiny state. While some reveled in victory and some wept in their whiskey, I sat at home wondering if I had made a terrible mistake.

I approve this message

Politicians are products. Have no illusions; be not romantic about Kennedy's Camelot or Reagan's Morning in America. Politicians are canned, packaged, marketed, bought and sold just like any other product, like ketchup (but they're more tart), like coffee (but they're sometimes even nuttier), or like Preparation-H (but they can have the opposite effect).

The only place where classic negative advertising is still practiced is in politics. Rarely on TV these days will we see something like the "Pepsi challenge" or "The Whopper beat the Big Mac" campaigns, one product calling out another and declaring superiority. When was the last time you saw a side-by-side comparison of how many more dishes Ivory can clean versus the "other leading brand"? Even batteries wimp out now, staking a position of *parity* instead of pre-eminence when they claim "Nothing outlasts the Energizer" or "Duracell: no battery is stronger, longer.'"

In political advertising, there is no hesitation about highlighting the deficiencies of the other "brands." It's so brazen, so cutthroat, that the FCC and the Federal Elections Commission require a real person – the candidate – to publicly take responsibility for the content of their broadcast advertising, saying they in fact "approved this message."

Imagine if we advertised other products the way we advertise in politics. Can you imagine an airline commercial that sounded like this:

(Background: ominous music under)

(Deep, menacing voice over) "Last year, more than 281 people lost their lives flying Go-Far Airlines. Boston: <u>28</u>! St. Louis: <u>71</u>! Ypsilanti: <u>119</u> innocent people killed, most of them frequent fliers; some of them orphans. Last year, more people died flying Go-Far Airlines than all other airlines combined. And how many more will die next year? When you choose to fly, fly with Sky-Time Air! Remember: *Sky-Time Air, when you really want to make it there alive.*"

If you wanted to kill the passenger airline industry in one day, run *that* commercial. Half the people would be afraid to fly any airline; the other half would be shocked and offended by Sky-Time's poor taste. Soon, the blowback would hit *every* airline and nobody would be flying. Bad for air travel – but good for Amtrak!

As ridiculous as it sounds, that's precisely the way politicians market themselves. Replace "Go-Far" and "Sky-Time" with "Republican" and "Democrat" or "incumbent" and "challenger," and you've got yourself a typical negative campaign commercial. But the effect on politics, government service, and civic participation in terms of voter turnout is just as damaging as that fictional airline ad. Politicians don't just throw mud; they throw acid. Negative campaigning has become a

---

* Except Robert Conrad. He was bad ass sticking that Eveready on his shoulder and daring you to call it a "regular battery." He'd rip that little pink bunny a new one if he had the chance.

cancer in the body politic, which leaves millions of people discouraged, disenfranchised, and disillusioned about democratic elections and the politicians who serve in government.

If negative campaigning is so bad, why is it still used? Because it *works*. If you heard a commercial that the leading brand of toothpaste actually *caused* cavities, you might know it was a lie. But if you heard it often enough, it would become hard for you to not start at least *considering* another brand.

How do I know so much about negative political ads? Well, I've made more than a few in my career and – right or wrong – most of them were pretty effective. The sad fact is negative advertising in politics – when done well – is a lot like a car accident on the highway. Nobody likes an accident, but everybody slows down to look.

The M&M's on Air Force One

In 1992, I signed on to be a media advisor for the re-election campaign of President George H.W. Bush. I had volunteered for Bush in 1988, but this was my first time helping craft the message. The Republican establishment was with the President, but he faced a serious primary challenge from the right by commentator Pat Buchanan. Bush's infamous "read my lips, no new taxes" line was being played over and over again by Buchanan's team. It was an amazing moment. That sound bite became ubiquitous (even my three-year-old son at the time was walking around the house sputtering, "Read my lips, no new taxes!") and everyone knew what it signified: that President Bush – at least as portrayed by Buchanan's ads – was a flip-flopper. Buchanan's ads used the President's own words lifted from his convention speech to make him a hypocrite on the issue of taxes. The message was clear, simple, and a good solid hit.

It's much easier working for the challenger than it is for the incumbent. An incumbent campaign may have a lot going for it (like money, friends, support, and name recognition), but it has a lot weighing it down. It's especially true in a state like New Hampshire where Primary voters expect genuine retail politics from their candidates. With an incumbent president, it's hard to move around. There are too many layers of consultants to go through. It is infinitely more complicated when the incumbent is a sitting president. There's the White House staff, the RNC, the campaign staff (local and national), the advance staff, and of course the Secret Service. Just getting access to the candidate is physically burdensome. It's hard for a politician to shake hands and kiss babies when the guys in dark suits and sunglasses are pushing people away.

On January 15, 1992, President Bush scheduled a swing through the Seacoast region of New Hampshire and we had all sorts of challenges to overcome*. The economy was down. Unemployment was up. A poll published the day before said that only forty-six percent of New Hampshire Republicans supported Bush. There was a chance the sitting President could lose the primary.

No Republican candidate could visit Portsmouth and not stop for a visit and a photograph with Evelyn Marconi. She was a City Councilor and the proud proprietor of Geno's Chowder shop, a great seafood, lunch joint, and lobster pound perched on stilts precariously teetering over Portsmouth Harbor. The walls of the establishment were covered with photos of Evelyn and her late husband, Geno, posing with virtually every Republican to run for office it seemed since the 1940s. The problem – and at the time this was just as politically sensitive as the Palestinian negotiations – was that the President was on Evelyn's shit list. This petite, matronly woman with a shock of gray hair would show her displeasure with GOP leaders by turning their pictures around on the wall. And at this moment in history, her photo with George Herbert Walker Bush was "turned around." Evelyn was a dyed-in-the-wool fiscal and social conservative and she was none too happy with Bush 41 for his raising taxes after publicly pledging he would not do so at the 1988 GOP convention.

In order to get Evelyn to turn the President's photo back around and to allow him to make a campaign stop at her restaurant, we had to do some horse trading. I was part of the Advance Team with Joel Maiola, a longtime friend and then-Chief of Staff to New Hampshire Governor

---

* Like: what the hell were we going to do with Quayle? Don't get me wrong. Dan Quayle is actually a very nice, very thoughtful guy. But when he was sent to campaign in NH, we didn't know where we could send him that wouldn't cause a problem. When George Bush announced Quayle as his running mate in 1988, he came off like a high school kid who just won prom king. He never recovered from that image, an image only made worse by the inevitable gaffes.

(and later, US Senator) Judd Gregg. He and I were dispatched to try to convince Evelyn that if she received Bush, then she could ride in the presidential motorcade that evening and get a tour of the then-new Air Force One with Bush himself.

Evelyn was tough. The President was welcome to do a drop by. She would round up plenty of local Republicans and she would be respectful, of course. And, yes, she would turn his picture around. But she intended to have a word with him about her displeasure during the brief motorcade ride later that evening on the way back to Pease Air Force Base to say goodbye. So we had a deal and the meet-and-greet was added to the President's schedule for the following week's trip.

The event at Geno's couldn't have gone any better. Evelyn was gracious and proudly showed the President his photo on the wall. The national press loved it. It was a positive color event which sent the clear message that President Bush was much loved by conservatives in the state. Later that evening Bush then went to Yoken's Restaurant and addressed 800 people from the Portsmouth Chamber of Commerce. After his speech Evelyn Marconi, along with two other elderly lady GOP activists, got invited to ride in the President's limo and drove to Pease Air Force base with him and Gregg. The ladies were having the time of their lives. I don't think Evelyn ever gave the President that piece of her mind she had promised.

A patrician figure, Bush 41 invited all three to board the new Air Force One. It was a gleaming 747 that still had the new plane smell. Once aboard, the women began to clean the plane out. They took playing cards, coffee mugs, and presidential boxes of M&M's, all with Bush's encouragement. They loved every minute of it. The President, ever the gracious, accommodating host, gave them cuff links and tie clips. It was a wonder the seats were still there when the plane went wheels up!

As the plane lifted off the tarmac into the cold night sky toward Washington, Evelyn – her arms filled with tchotchkes – commented on what a very nice man the President was, and in spite of a difference here and there, how much she liked him. I knew President Bush had converted her back to the team, but he couldn't give M&M's to every Republican and Independent in the state. That's when I knew we had a problem.

Running in place

I worked with the brilliant young political strategist Mike Murphy and we got along famously*. Mike had been a *wunderkind* on Bob Dole's 1988 campaign and was brought in from Washington to be a media consultant for the Bush re-election effort. Even though he was a "D.C. guy," he had the down-to-earth temperament, incredible intellect, and sense of humor that made him a superior operative both on the ground and in the editing room. Mike is to this day one of the smartest and most creative political media guys I've ever met and we have remained good friends. Truth be told, the Bush presidential re-election campaign was really being steered by Washington. They weren't on the ground in New Hampshire and Iowa, and they weren't hearing what Mike and I and Joel and so many others were hearing first hand: that Buchanan was making huge inroads against the President in his upstart challenge. Our guy just wasn't connecting with the people. And the voters were not happy.

At one point, President Bush addressed a joint session of the New Hampshire Legislature in the statehouse chamber in Concord. His speech, while not bad, gave his detractors (on both sides) the opportunity to grumble their displeasure. Bush was boxed in on what he could say; he couldn't even mention taxes lest he open himself to further criticism. After the speech, Bob Teeter, the President's former pollster and then campaign manager, turned to me and said, "I think that went very well, don't you?" I was stunned. Teeter was a smart operator, but these Washington guys just couldn't see it. They were in complete and utter denial.

While the Washington headquarters' position on Buchanan was to not engage him, not to dignify his campaign by even acknowledging its existence, Mike and I tried to make some ads that would slow Buchanan's momentum. We stood on a street corner in the middle of a colder-than-normal winter day with a camera crew asking real people

---

* Mike and I stumbled into the President's hotel late one night, punch drunk from fatigue. The Secret Service had their black SUV war wagons in place, the kind with the bubble top and machine gun posts. Mike took one look at the firepower and remarked, "Holy shit, they must have seen our poll numbers from last night!"

if we could talk to them about the President. Some people laughed at us, some people yelled, a few even flipped us the bird. But we were able to find some people* who supported Bush. Among them was a little old man with a thick Canadian accent who said everyone called him "The Mayor." The title of course was only honorary – but at whatever social club he belonged to that apparently was what his friends called him, because according to him, "I know everyone."

"That Mr. Buchanan, I don't know about him," "The Mayor" said in his Pidgin English, shaking his head. "I just don't trust him."

Mike cut together a spot with the footage. We'd have a clip of someone saying something positive about Bush, then go to a cut of "The Mayor" shaking his head and expressing his doubts about Buchanan. The commercial was powerful and accomplished what the campaign had yet been unable to do: undercut Buchanan. But the Mayor gave it some humor; it was not mean, just provided voters with a little doubt about Buchanan's temperament to be the leader of the Free World. Mike showed me the rough cut and I thought it was great!

Mike and I presented the ad, which we called "The Mayor," to Bush's senior campaign team in Washington. (It seems that everyone but *me* knew that Bush's advisor Mary Matalin was sleeping with Clinton's senior advisor James Carville, a fact I found somewhat troubling – especially having witnessed Mary's apparent disengagement with what was happening in NH.) Washington dismissed the ad out of hand. They thought the President was doing fine and still didn't want to engage Buchanan. They were mistaking motion for progress. As the late former New Hampshire Governor Hugh Gregg said in his book about the campaign, the whole team was unfortunately "running in place." I was stunned that no one seemed to get that we were in real trouble. I respected and admired the President. Judd Gregg and many others had a lot on the line for the guy. It was important for Bush and the party that we win in NH. I wanted to end Buchanan's bid here – but it was looking more doubtful each day the Primary crept closer.

---

* These have to be *real* people. Your advertising gland immediately starts tingling when pretty, well-dressed, articulate people smoothly rattle off campaign talking points. Actors will not do. And paid staffers, though probably unpolished enough to appear credible, are exposés waiting to happen. Some reporter or campaign operative will track down the not-so-random "man on the street" and reveal him or her to be a plant.

The wrong optic

At the end of the 1992 New Hampshire Presidential Primary, President Bush scheduled a final visit to the state. Buchanan's people clearly had the momentum. Their candidate would appear on college campuses and walk to the town dump with a pack of true believers, all of whom smelled blood, with an excited gaggle of local, national, and international press in tow. They called themselves the "Buchanan Brigades" and Pat himself liked to call his campaign an uprising, a revolution. His supporters were "the peasants with pitchforks."

The Bush campaign on the other hand had a hard time finding appropriate venues. They did "safe" events, safe politically speaking.

In order to accommodate the size of the President's entourage and field a respectable crowd, the entire Bedford Mall needed to be closed down. While Bush made his way through the rope line shaking hands and autographing campaign signs, a man named Roger Ham from Ridgefield Park, NJ reached out and grabbed the President's hand, pulled him into the crowd, and wouldn't let him go.

"When are you going to let [Lyndon] LaRouche out of jail?" Ham yelled. The Secret Service quickly broke his hold and coming from every direction dragged Ham away. I certainly was relieved no harm came to the President, but I found the whole encounter emblematic of the Bush campaign in New Hampshire at that moment. The President, locked in the bubble of incumbency, was too insulated, too cut off from the real world. Watching a man get dragged away from the campaigning President was just the wrong optic. But Bush, unfazed, just moved on, still smiling and working the crowd.

It's local, stupid

The night of the New Hampshire primary – February 18, 1992 – the mood at Bush campaign headquarters at the Center of New Hampshire hotel ballroom was tense as the first returns began to come in. Early exit polling in the day looked quite grim and by the time the polls closed at 8:00 pm Buchanan and the President were neck and neck. Bush eventually pulled away and won the contest fifty-three to thirty-seven percent, but it wasn't the comfortable victory that Bush needed to quell Buchanan or quiet the national press. We won, but according to the press coverage, we really lost.

By February 18th, the national campaign had already moved on to South Carolina – mentally if not actually physically. It was there that they were planning their Southern "firewall." The New Hampshire victory speech was given, not by Bush who remained in Washington, but by senior advisor and Washington super-lobbyist Charlie Black. Black was the ultimate Washington insider and while he is bright, well regarded, and highly respected in GOP circles, Black only re-enforced the Bush campaign as being Washington through and through. What an elbow to New Hampshire! "Bush might as well have just sent a telegram saying 'thanks for nothing,'" said one county chairman as he left the ballroom.

Could Pat Buchanan have been stopped in New Hampshire? Even with the conservative firebrand getting all sorts of weighted support from the *Union Leader*, I think he could have. Tip O'Neill said, "All politics is local." Former New Hampshire Governor Hugh Gregg said, "All elections are local." Had the Bush campaign been more focused on running in New Hampshire – as opposed to running a national campaign – they could have done better. Perhaps the ghosts of the 1988 Willie Horton ad still haunted them. Maybe if they had run the "Mayor" ad and concentrated on more hyper-local campaign initiatives, Buchanan's numbers could have been far enough in Bush's rearview mirror that the President could have turned his attention sooner to the changing Democratic field (and a new frontrunner named Bill Clinton).

In any event, I still hold George H.W. Bush (aka Bush 41) as a fine man. I really liked the guy and viewed him as a statesman and a man with the experience, temperament, and gravitas to deserve another term. I was disappointed that come November the President would lose his re-election bid to the young upstart governor of Arkansas.

The man from plaid

For the 1996 race, I knew some pretty powerful Republicans were going to give it a try: people like Bob Dole, Phil Gramm, maybe even

California Governor Pete Wilson or General Colin Powell. I was asked to attend a meeting at the office of my longtime friend and former New Hampshire Attorney General (and Republican Godfather) Tom Rath. He was introducing the former Governor of Tennessee to a small group of Republican activists so I agreed to attend. Lamar Alexander was a slow-talking, very bright Southerner who had served two terms as governor and as Education Secretary for President Bush. He had a compelling message. I listened to his talk and took a copy of his book*, but I wasn't really enamored with him at the time.

I definitely didn't want to work for Buchanan after what he did to Bush in '92. Bob Dole looked like the establishment candidate, which meant he was going to be the Bush campaign all over again: the staff was filled with consultants and the Washington establishment who were running the thing from the get-go. Rath (who had worked for Dole in 1988) continued to work on me, trying to convince me that Alexander would be a more interesting and compelling opportunity. At one point I flew to Tennessee to meet with Lamar and Honey Alexander at their place at Blackberry Farm in the great Smoky Mountains. I spent the weekend with some interesting national Republican leaders and fundraisers including Ted Welch, the Tennessee businessman who had raised millions for Reagan and Bush, not to mention plenty of other Republicans as well.

I ultimately decided to join the Alexander team because they were the guys who wanted me and frankly seemed to have a significant role for me to play. Some of the best political minds (Rath, Bill Cahill, and the aforementioned Mike Murphy) were already onboard and it would be a chance to play a more significant role than I had played with Bush. I also had a feeling that this campaign was going to be fun – and with a little luck – Alexander might just steal early momentum from Dole the insider and from Buchanan on the ideological Right.

---

* *Everyone* who ran for president had to have a book. Alexander's was called *Six Months Off*, Dole's was *American Dreams*, Buchanan's was *Right From the Beginning*. Steve Forbes didn't have a book, but he didn't need one. He had a whole damn magazine!

I'm walkin'

Alexander's name recognition in New Hampshire was almost nothing. During one early New Hampshire radio interview, he was introduced by the local news guy as "Governor Alexander Lamar." Even though Alexander had been in public life for some time, he was essentially a blank page having never run for national office. We used the opportunity to define Alexander on our terms. Playing on the party's distain for the federal government, we'd remind voters that "governors are outside of Washington." They were chief executives who made tough decisions, balanced budgets, and didn't get mired down in legislation. When someone would challenge Alexander's outsider status because he had served in the Bush Administration he'd quip he had been in Washington only "long enough to get vaccinated, but not infected." I always loved that line.

I always say, "Before they can vote for you, they gotta like you. Before they like you, they gotta know you." Alexander had the ability to raise money which would enable him to build a stronger-than-anticipated campaign team and, more importantly, allow the Governor to get on TV early, getting a jump in name ID over some of the other candidates who were even more unknown than he was. The early ads (produced by Mike Murphy) introduced Alexander to the state.

There was nothing flashy about Lamar Alexander. Some found him downright boring. I didn't find him so. I thought he was deeply intellectual, but also a crafty politician. There were a lot of layers to Lamar and I had a sense as voters got to peel them back, that the more they got to know him, the more they would grow to like and respect him.

One of the successful campaign techniques Alexander used while running for Governor was his "Walk Across Tennessee." Then-strategist Doug Bailey helped him come up with the idea. The image of Alexander in a red plaid shirt walking the road was familiar to Tennessee voters. We all thought he should do the same thing in New Hampshire. I came up with Alexander's walk theme: "From Concord to Manchester to the Sea." The Washington press corps thought it was a silly parlor trick. It wasn't. Not only did it provide the media with access and great photo ops, but it provided New Hampshire voters with a real opportunity to meet the candidate on their terms – in their towns. Besides, Bob Dole wouldn't walk anywhere- so Lamar's relative youth and vitality was a good contrast to all those guys in suits! At first, the walks (done in several mile segments over a series of months) were sparsely attended, but by the end of the race there were large crowds walking with the man in the plaid shirt.

Lamar would keep track of how many horn honks, thumbs up, and middle fingers he'd get along the way. At first, there was little to no reaction from the passing traffic. As we went on and the campaign built momentum the honks got more frequent, and more passionate. Soon the crowds were getting big and we started to need police escorts. Elite Washington political writers would fly in to New Hampshire, dine at fancy restaurants, then drive a rental car fifty miles to meet up with us and walk a mile or so among the great unwashed masses of real voters "to get a feel" for the campaign. It made them get out of the office and feel like reporters again. They also got to see the Governor in action. The press coverage was good. Lamar Alexander was new, engaged in retail politics, close to New Hampshire voters, and unafraid to slowly build political capital mile by mile, town by town.

Flattened

Dole was too old, Buchanan was too extreme, Phil Gramm was an arrogant Texan who would surely self-implode. Lamar Alexander was just right. Moreover, as we got closer to the New Hampshire primary, polls showed Alexander was favored by a significant number of voters. Among those who were with someone else, Alexander seemed to be everyone else's *second* choice. "I like Dole, but if I didn't vote for him I'd vote for Alexander," was a common verbatim that showed up in our polling. By the summer of 1995, we'd gone from nowhere in the polls to third place, closely behind Dole and Buchanan. This was a bit of a miracle for a guy who had not that long ago been introduced to New Hampshire as "Alexander Lamar."

We in the campaign dubbed ourselves "Alexander's Band." And in many ways, we began to resemble a well-rehearsed lounge act. The Governor would get up, give a well-reasoned speech as to why he – not

Dole, not Buchanan – could beat then-President Bill Clinton. "It's easy as A-B-C," he'd say. "Alexander Beats Clinton." Then he'd play a little piano*, sign some books, and more often than not win over the crowd.

In September of 1995, multimillionaire publishing heir Steve Forbes decided to enter the presidential race. He had two things going for him: 1) his advocacy of the easy-to-understand flat tax, and 2) $25 million dollars of his own money to throw at the campaign. Forbes quickly became the flavor of the month. He stirred up real discussion about the flat tax; every other candidate found themselves responding to questions about Forbes' plan. But Forbes was a one-trick pony; everything was "flat tax." Alexander needed to get out from underneath this issue. Forbes knew he couldn't catch Dole or Buchanan in NH, so he systematically went gunning for Alexander and third place. In the debates and forums, Forbes would whack Lamar, then Lamar began to hit back. We knew people wouldn't be psyched about a flat tax if they knew the details: that they would lose their home mortgage interest deductions or their charitable gift deductions. Alexander showed the field that Forbes had a glass jaw and couldn't take a punch. He also exposed Forbes as a megalomaniac billionaire with a chip in the back of his head who could do nothing but say, "flat tax, flat tax, flat tax," again and again.

Our crowds continued to build, as did the excitement for the campaign. It was great fun, a great team, and – frankly – a great candidate! We did everything right on the Alexander campaign, except win. We had a man with no name recognition in New Hampshire and Iowa who several months later came in a close third place in a tight three-way race with a large field. Alexander received twenty-three percent of the vote, right behind Buchanan and Dole who got twenty-seven and twenty-six percent respectively. Forbes was a distant fourth with twelve percent, while Richard Lugar, Alan Keyes, Morry Taylor and Bob Dornan finished in single digits. With Buchanan having little credible support among mainstream Republicans in the rest of the country, many analysts predicted it was now a two-man race between Dole and Alexander for the heart and soul of the Republican Party.

---

* Lamar learned to play piano at the age of four and excelled in both country and classical music.

After the New Hampshire primary, I continued to serve the campaign, coordinating the New England states for Super Tuesday, but the national money and support for Alexander dried up not long after New Hampshire. After Bill Clinton defeated Dole for re-election in 1996, I had a bunch of bumper stickers printed up and mailed to political reporters across the country. They said only "2000!" the date floating over a background of familiar red plaid[*]. I didn't know for sure that Alexander would run again – but this little bumper sticker sure got the chattering class in Washington and beyond talking. Observing the woes of Clinton's second term, sensing the incredible battle fatigue felt by Republicans and Democrats alike, I thought going into the 2000 race that the GOP had an excellent chance of winning back the White House.

Breaking up is hard to do

I really thought it was important to be with the right candidate, one who could close the deal. The quality of *electability* became central to my decision making process.

After the 1996 race, I stayed in touch with Lamar Alexander. I worked on Alexander's PAC, The Campaign for a New American Century. I still greatly admired him, but my attention was steadily turning toward then-Texas Governor George W. Bush. The eldest son of my first presidential client was getting a lot of buzz. The younger Bush had won re-election in Texas with a record sixty-nine percent of the vote. He was raising ungodly amounts of campaign money, sucking the oxygen out of the would-be campaigns of Dan Quayle and Elizabeth Dole.

I had dinner with Mike Murphy in Washington at our old hangout: Sam & Harry's Steakhouse on 19th [†]. He didn't want to work for another Bush. And, although he liked and respected Alexander, he and many others felt that that dog would simply not hunt this time – especially

---

[*] Lamar was not behind the stickers, which got considerable ink with the politico press. The Governor was too much of a Southern gentleman. He thought it impolite and presumptuous to do such a thing. I thought, "Fuck it. Let's do it anyway."

[†] Sam & Harry's did not pay for a mention in this book; however, if they'd like to spiff me a steak next time I'm in town I would not object.

with Governor Bush and Senator John McCain both in the race. Mike had gotten to know McCain pretty well and greatly respected the Arizona Senator as a maverick war hero with a compelling personal and political narrative.

"Don't go working for Bush," he warned me. "It's going to be a clusterfuck of Washington and Austin consultants. It'll be just like the last Bush you worked for." Then he offered, "Why don't you help run things for McCain in New Hampshire?" I had to say no. Many of my political clients, friends, and mentors were already on board with Bush and urging me to do the same. But I was still – for now at least – formally committed to Alexander and after our meeting I felt a little like I was cheating on my wife.

After a couple of weeks of soul searching[*], I realized I simply couldn't support Alexander in 2000. My heart wasn't in it. I wanted to tell the Governor face-to-face, so I decided I should go to Nashville and meet with him. I owed him that. My plan was to fly down, meet Alexander at his office or at my hotel, and explain my reasoning.

When I arrived at the Loews Vanderbilt Hotel in Nashville the night before our scheduled meeting, there was a message waiting for me at the front desk that the Governor was coming to pick me up the next morning at 8:30 am to bring me to his house for our meeting. I was expecting some staffer from the PAC would be waiting for me in the lobby. Instead it was Lamar Alexander himself.

We drove in his car the 15 minutes from downtown to his Nashville home and he invited me inside. It was one of the hardest conversations I ever had. I felt like I was breaking up with my girlfriend. "Lamar I can't do for you this time what I did in '96. I don't have the passion or the energy." It was uncomfortable, especially because he was going to have to drive me back to my hotel[†]. But Alexander couldn't have been more of a gentleman about it. He officially dropped out of the race in August of 1999, after poor fundraising and a weak showing in an early Iowa straw poll.

---

[*]   Apparently, I had one to search.

[†]   It's one thing to break up with your girlfriend. It's another to do it in her house and then ask her for a ride home after the deed is done.

Now serving as a US Senator from Tennessee, Lamar Alexander has become a well-regarded and highly respected voice in the Republican Party. He is a class act and a true statesman.

Great Expectations

The George W. Bush campaign needed another media consultant like it needed more cowboy boots. But my longtime friend, client, and mentor, now-Senator Judd Gregg, insisted that Karl Rove bring me aboard. "We'd love to have you," Rove would say in distracted, hurried phone calls to me, then proceeded to ignore the idea for several weeks. When the phone didn't ring, I knew it was Rove.

The first time I met Governor Bush was at a campaign stop at my son's elementary school. I wasn't part of the crew yet, but I suggested the location for the event and photo op to Joel Maiola, Gregg's longtime political aide and Chief of Staff, who was officially coordinating things in New Hampshire for Bush. I was told to wait outside of the Peter Woodbury Elementary School in Bedford, next to Bush's campaign bus with a couple of wags for what's known as a brief "meet and greet." As he was coming out of the school into the bright sunlight, someone tapped him on the shoulder and turned him toward me. "Governor, this is Pat Griffin. He's going to be helping us out." Bush grabbed my hand hard and got right up in my face. You got the distinct feeling he was taking your pulse. "Griffy, nice to meet ya. I heard a lot about ya," he said in that voice so frequently parodied on Saturday Night Live. Some in the media like to suggest Bush was a dumb cowboy, but that's not the man I rode around New Hampshire with. I found then-Governor Bush to be gregarious, engaged, and bright. He was much smarter than he ever came across on TV. He knew the issues well and the family business of politics was clearly in his blood. I immediately liked the guy.

In order to seal the deal I had to meet with Karen Hughes, Bush's fiercely loyal communications director. The campaign was going to be making a November 2, 1999 stop in the far northern town of Gorham, NH. That day I drove the 143 miles from Boston to the Town & Country Inn for the Northern White Mountains Chamber of Commerce luncheon event at which Bush was to keynote.

"Pat, Karen Hughes. Really pleased to meet you." Hughes was one of the most imposing figures – man or woman – I think I ever came across in politics. She stood six feet tall, had size 12 shoes, and a handshake tighter than any NBA forward. "While the Governor speaks, let's go for a walk on the golf course and talk."

On a cold, drizzling October afternoon in the North Country, the last thing I wanted to do was take a walk on a golf course. The grey skies looked like they were dropped in from the Land of Oz. In hindsight it may have been an omen. Hughes' stride was so long I had trouble keeping up with her. After the third hole, I had thoroughly pitched myself and Hughes formally welcomed me aboard. I would help place local media for the campaign and work on crafting the message for "W" in the first-in-the-nation primary state. As I drove back from the North Country to my office in Manchester, I was excited. But the storm clouds remained dark and threatening. That night we had a horrific snow and wind storm – there was even lightning! An omen indeed because little did I know there would be many more storm clouds on the horizon in the months to come.

Woke up this morning, got yourself a gun

What I soon learned was that the Texas political mob is tighter than the Sopranos and just as dangerous. I found myself in the middle of yet another "Imperial" campaign, one with as little flexibility and deftness as that of an actual White House incumbent. The marching orders were coming out of Austin. Just like his father's in 1992, George W. Bush's campaign was not plugged into what was happening on the streets of New Hampshire. When he first visited the state, Bush was at sixty-three percent in the polls. John McCain, who spent his days in real town hall meetings talking to real people, was slowly cutting into that lead.

One of Bush's closest advisers was his Texas Chief of Staff Joe Allbaugh, a huge roast beef of a guy, who stood 6' 3" and had a tight military hair cut. With Rove and Hughes, Allbaugh made up the so-called "Iron Triangle" around Bush. One day, on which we drove him from the airport to his hotel in Manchester, Allbaugh turned to Joel Maiola and me and said, "You know, if you guys could just win this thing here, it'd all be over." I thought, *If you guys would just give us a chance, maybe we could.*

Governor Bush had been coasting right through the primary campaign, one safe event after another. Then on November 5th, WHDH TV reporter Andy Hiller gave Bush a pop quiz on the names of four world leaders in current hot spots[*]. Let's just say the then-Governor's answer to who the current leader of Pakistan was didn't sit well. Bush stammered, "The new Pakistani general, he's just been elected - not elected, this guy took over office. It appears this guy is going to bring stability to the country and I think that's good news for the subcontinent." The next day, a poll showed Bush's lead over McCain in New Hampshire has shrunk to within eight points. From then on, the unfair image of Bush as a petulant, entitled buffoon was born and just continued to grow.

The campaign circled its wagons after that. It was even tougher behind the scenes to get through to the inner circle. Everyone was tense, on guard. The prestigious and infamous *New York Times* writer, the late R. W. "Johnny" Apple, was scheduled to fly to New Hampshire and interview the Governor on the campaign bus. Apple had been the bureau chief for the *Times* in Saigon, London, Moscow, and Washington, but at this point late in his career he was traveling the world writing mostly about food and fine wine. There was much handwringing and teeth gnashing among the Austin mob in anticipation of how the old scribe from the nation's most liberal newspaper might try to foil Bush. Someone getting on the campaign bus noticed the palaver among Bush, Rove, Hughes, and Allbaugh, and wondered aloud what was up. Bush's chairman Judd Gregg, who is nonplussed by these kinds of situations[†]

---

[*] The story of the pop quiz later appeared in over 100 US newspapers and was replayed endlessly on network and cable TV. I'm not an apologist for GWB by any means, but in the days after the story, the piece was roundly criticized by fellow journalists who called it "unfair," "gotcha journalism," an "ambush," and (pun intended) "bush league."

[†] If ever I met a person who better exemplified the Rudyard Kipling line about being able to "walk with kings – nor lose the common touch," it would be Judd Gregg. He came from a famous New Hampshire political family, but remains after 30 years in public service (in Congress, as a Governor, and then a US Senator) fundamentally unaffected and completely unpretentious. I've worked with Judd on his gubernatorial and US Senate campaigns. I'm heartened by the fact Judd and his wife Kathy could have been inhabitants of Washington for so long without becoming creatures of the place. Judd is a true statesman who's not afraid to say what's on his mind, as he did

and who was feeling as frustrated as the rest of us, said dryly (as is his style), "Oh, they're all worried about some food critic from the *New York Times*." It was the first laugh I had in weeks!

Expressly straight talked

There was a reluctance to engage John McCain in New Hampshire, much the same way Bush 41 had decided to ignore Pat Buchanan in 1992. McCain was continuing the kind of in-the-trenches, authentic retail politicking that I knew Mike Murphy would insist he do. Meantime, I wasn't making any friends on the Bush bus because I was challenging too much too often. I'd suggest we do something differently, question why we weren't doing something else. All of the New Hampshire advisors were begging Bush to do some live local radio talk shows. Karl Rove was outwardly dismissive of anything I – or most anyone else on the ground – suggested. His attitude was, *Place your ads and don't make waves, kid. You're lucky to be on this gravy train.*

After the Hiller debacle, Rove was worried about exposing Bush to too many interviews and too many crack-pot commentators with their own pop quiz questions at the ready. Specifically, Rove didn't want to get into a prolonged examination of Bush's position on abortion, which in some ways was becoming problematic. Bush had always been pro-life except in cases of rape, incest, or when the life of the mother was at stake. While this satisfied most Republicans, a large number of conservatives weren't sure he meant it. They distrusted him as they had his father.

McCain, who seemed to enjoy the actual sparring, was doing all the media he could, even outside of traditional news programming. He'd spend up to an hour at local radio stations during morning or afternoon drive time, national media in tow, taking song requests or answering questions like, "Ginger or Marianne?"* McCain was very good at taking questions and comments unfiltered from anyone who called in or any reporter with a pop quiz. He knew his stuff and was not

---

when he "dressed down" President Obama's budget director Peter Orszag on matters of fiscal restraint and common sense. Unfortunately, Judd Gregg is a breed of public servant that is all too rare in Washington these days.

* McCain said "Ginger," which isn't surprising because he was in the Navy.

afraid to tell people what he thought about substantive policy. In fact, McCain's "Straight Talk Express" was a come-as-you-are, open door to the local and national media. There was near-unfettered access to the gregarious Senator, who drank coffee, offered doughnuts, and answered all questions – no holds barred.

There could not be a greater contrast between McCain's lovefest with the media and Bush's campaign bus, in which the candidate was virtually sequestered from the media most days. The press resented it and it showed in their coverage of Bush.

After much cajoling from Gregg, Congressman Charlie Bass, and from other New Hampshire advisors, the Austin cabal finally agreed to let Bush do some live morning drive-time radio interviews. The Governor would call the stations from the campaign bus while it was en route to an event. With the help of Scott Tranchemontage, my former political media wiz who had extraordinary relationships with the local and national press, we presented a list of stations and reporters that the Governor should speak with whenever we had some available phone time.

I sat next to Bush in the front of the bus on a cold metal folding chair and dialed the studio numbers Scott had advanced on my cell phone. I'd fill Bush in on the name of the interviewer and what market the station was in. "Yep, yep," Bush replied, as he was prone to impatience. "Please hold for the Governor," I'd tell the producer, then pass the phone. Bush would then tap-dance his way through a series of mostly softball questions, with a few policy questions, that he generally handled well and allowed him the chance to interact directly with local media. The Governor was knowledgeable and likable and I began to think this would work.

"I don't want to deal with any questions on abortion," Bush said to me flatly. I explained if someone asked him about that he should deal with it the way he always had. "Okay," he said dismissively looking out the window of the bus, his black cowboy boots propped up on a railing in front of his swivel chair. "You're the smart guy."

The radio calls were going well until we did the interview with a station in Keene, NH staffed by a local political nutcase. Bush began, "Good morning. I'm fine. Glad to be with you. We're drivin' around New Hampshire trying to meet as many voters as we can and I'm askin' for the vote...what's that?... abortion?" Bush turned to me and gave me a stare I won't soon forget. It was same *enfant terrible* puss he'd make when he was tired or when he didn't get his hour of daily exercise. The call degenerated into a morass. The interviewer would not let up. In advertising terms, the crusading reporter was destroying "the product" right before my eyes and "the product" was pissed off at me.

After the call, Bush looked at me with what I can only describe as "The Texas Death Stare." This was a guy who had denied clemency to 152 convicted death row inmates during his terms as Governor[*]. So when it came to death stares, "W" knew how to put on his game face! He tossed the cell phone at me and I caught it after bobbling it a bit. "That went pretty well," Bush sneered. "What's next, smart guy?"[†] The days of unfettered media access to candidate Bush were now officially over and I was relegated – literally – to the back of the Bush bus with a number of other advisors and staff. At least I didn't have to sit on that cold metal chair again.

Slip sliding away

The day before the primary vote was a snowy one and New Hampshire schools were closed because of the storm. Sensing there had to be a better photo op than another controlled speech at some insurance company, Joel suggested (along with a few other local advisors) that the Governor should go sledding. The plan would be to dress Bush down in a winter coat, make him look like the regular guy (which he was), and get him to sit in a toboggan or inner tube and slide down Bragdon Farm Hill in Amherst with a bunch of kids (we knew that place would be packed with a lot of Republicans as Amherst was the mother lode for GOP voters). Bush showed up in his overcoat and suit, his cowboy boots leaving deep heel marks in the snow. The media pack around him was enormous, which made it hard for him to actually talk to voters.

---

[*] Not that I disagree with then-Governor Bush's policy on capital punishment. I just didn't want to meet "Old Sparky" myself, especially sitting in that cold metal chair!

[†] I would later recount this incident for *Newsweek*, saying that Bush had acted just like my 10 year old son. In the subsequent 8 years, I never got an invitation to the White House Christmas Party. Go figure!

Reporter Anne Kornblut, at the time from the *Boston Globe*, pulled me aside and asked pointedly why a man running for president needed to go sledding. It was a serious question about campaign tactics and political theater. I called it the "Elvis factor" or the "rock star factor."

"It's color. It helps us win on personality. I've never seen John McCain without a coat and tie on." I told Kornblut we were doing plenty of speeches on policy. George W. Bush is a good guy, down-to-earth, and a natural campaigner. "Winning New Hampshire is as much about liking the candidate, about connecting with voters, as it is about the issues.

"Besides," I said, "It's a snow day in New Hampshire – have some fun."

Later, someone asked Rove about my comment on clothing, color events, and image. "That's not what this campaign is about," Rove snapped at me. Later, on another campaign stop, Rove pulled me aside and scolded me. "Pat! Message: it's about issues – stay on it."

Later that night, the Bush campaign's national press secretary Ari Fleischer debated Mike Murphy of the McCain camp on CNN's "Crossfire" in a battle of the surrogates. The host, Bill Press, brought up my *Boston Globe* quote. "Is this true?" he asked Fleischer, "are we having a wardrobe war here?"

With that, Fleischer disavowed me. "Pat Griffin does not speak for the Bush campaign."

"I don't know why they're bashing their own guy," Murphy said. "I've worked with Pat Griffin before. He's a smart guy*." Murphy went on to say I was right, that George W. Bush was looking like an establishment candidate who walked around New Hampshire in a bubble wearing a suit and tie (even though McCain had been in Washington for more than 20 years. Nice spin, Murph!). He reminded Press and Fleischer that McCain had done over 100 town hall meetings all over the state and was out there among the people, busy all-day every-day joy riding with media, answering the tough questions.

I – who was too busy working for candidate Bush the night before the primary to watch television – got a cell phone call from a Bush staffer whom I liked and respected who had seen the exchange on

---

* Thanks Murph. At least the McCain campaign was on my side!

CNN. "Ari Fleischer just fucked you on national television," he said. Nice, very nice.

After the broadcast, I met Murphy for a drink. "They did a number on *you*," he said sympathetically as I sipped a beer. He passed on some overnight polling data from the McCain campaign, the campaign I had turned down a chance to be a part of. The poll showed McCain beating Bush by at least ten points, likely much more. I was stunned. Not only were we going to lose in a huge way, but the team I worked so hard for had just kicked me in the teeth on national television.

On Primary Day, after driving to some polling places early in the morning with the Bush entourage, I waited with the rest of the team at our campaign bunker at the Residence Inn in Merrimack, NH. Sometime around mid-day Joel Maiola received a call with the early exit poll numbers. "That bad?" I heard him ask incredulously into his cell phone.

Later I found myself alone in Rove's suite. He was sitting at the kitchen counter, typing away on his laptop. The bed and other amenities in the room appeared untouched. I presumed this suite was procured solely for the purpose of housing Rove's incredibly large brain and that he had domiciled in a different room somewhere down the hall.

"I don't think we were able to pull it off for you today," I humbly said. McCain was about to win New Hampshire by nineteen percentage points.

"Don't worry," Rove said without ever looking up from his laptop. "We'll get 'em." Then Rove said matter-of-factly that they'd be able to do in South Carolina what we couldn't get done up here.

I knew then that Karl Rove had already "moved on." Whether it was that morning or a week or two earlier, he had mentally "checked out" of New Hampshire long ago and was already looking to South Carolina, where another firewall had been carefully put into place.

What happened next was the nastiest campaign I had ever seen. I'm no Pollyanna when it comes to running tough political ads, but what was done to John McCain, his wife, and his children was despicable. It was in fact racist. It was unbecoming. It's hard to hold Bush blameless for South Carolina, but a campaign stratagem that disgusting could only have been crafted by as fundamentally Machiavellian an individual as Rove. While many of the most offensive attacks launched against

McCain were done allegedly by "third parties," the media and the chattering class in Washington saw the fine hand of Karl Christian Rove. Twisted genius that he is, he was more than just a clever Svengali carefully managing his brand. Karl Rove is representative of a certain type of soulless gargoyle whose megalomania and absolute quest for power would make even Rasputin blush. In the end, Bush won South Carolina fifty-three to forty-two percent. In politics, nice guys unfortunately sometimes do finish last.

The goal of the Bush campaign had never been to run a local campaign in New Hampshire. They were built for running a national campaign, one which they very nearly lost. Another primary, another establishment candidate over-handled, over-consulted, seriously insulated and out-of-touch with voters.

The moral of the story is

Politicians are products, the same as ketchup or cars or doughnut holes. Expectations for all products must be met or exceeded; managing expectations can be the difficult thing. In order for voters to commit to a candidate, they need to engage the candidate.

Howard Dean showed the world how to use the Internet to raise money. Barack Obama took it to the next level, using social media techniques to organize and coordinate campaign activities and micro-segment communications to his supporters. Now, potential governors, mayors, and town dog catchers are setting up Facebook pages to build a following. Someday, we may even use our laptops or iPhones to cast our ballots. (Think that would drive up turn-out a bit?)

Though I still enjoy political consulting for state and federal offices, I don't think I'll ever consult for a presidential campaign again. I skipped 2008 in order to be a Republican commentator for a number of local, regional, and cable TV stations and I had a blast. I was in every way a free agent and I could say whatever I thought. It was for me the first presidential campaign of my life that was both exhilarating and liberating.

While we're on the subject of "never agains," I don't think I could ever fly Go-Far Airlines again. After all, didn't you hear what Sky-Time said about them in their last ad?

Chapter twelve

So Now What?

The future of advertising – the order is rapidly fadin'

Yogi Berra once said, "The future ain't what it used to be." Today we know he was right.

For those of us who had dreamed of space travel, world peace, and mass marketing, we now know all too well the limits of our potential. There will never be vacations on the moon, nutritious meals in pill form, or domesticated apes working as our slaves (but quietly planning their revolt once they get the ability to speak). Heck, even the dream of getting the Beatles back together is soured because when they did so in 1995 with "Free as a Bird" it just reminded us how it could "never be."*

The world is going to evolve rapidly and we'll all be witnesses to it. As Bob Dylan said of the changing times, prophesize with your pen but "don't speak too soon for the wheel's still in spin and there's no telling who it is naming." At the risk of choosing the loser who "will be later to win," here's what the times have in store for us on the marketing innovations front:

The first one now will later be last

After years of dire warnings and predictions of their demise, the death of the newspaper is finally upon us, as previously stated. Like a mighty athlete now infirmed and unable to function, the once mighty

---

* Personally, I still blame Yoko Ono.

newspapers now lie on their own deathbeds. This is not necessarily a reflection on the quality of journalism, nor the lack of need for a healthy, functional free press. There are many fine papers (and journalists) still out there, and as I've stated, we are all still addicted to content. But subscribing to a newspaper is teetotaling compared to the robust avenues of information at one's fingertips. It's like *The Shining's* Jack Toland being locked in the Overlook Hotel's barroom and sipping from the kitchen sherry instead of the top shelf scotch.

It's the end of newspapers because as the least technological of the mass media, they will be the first to go. All the news content a paper produces is already outdated by the time it's thrown off the back of the diesel-belching delivery van at 5:00 am, never mind the time that ticks by while it sits on your front stoop. Papers are in an economic death spiral. Even if reader circulation were to stop plummeting, papers would still collapse under the weight of their own infrastructures. The vigorous commercial marketplace, that once provided dozens of car dealerships, department stores, banks, and other hometown advertisers to support the local newspaper, has been consolidated or outright dried up. There isn't the money around to pay the writers (let alone the copy-setters, press operators, truck drivers, and circulation managers needed to crank any tab out in a 24 hour period). When you can't pay the writers, there's nothing left of value in the paper*. The content writers will go elsewhere, just as their readers already have. Look for the best writers in the coming year online: Politico, Slate, TMZ, PerezHilton.com, CNN.com, ESPN.com, MSNBC.com, FoxNews.com. Sarah Palin's blog?

Book 'em, Dan-o

Libraries will be the next to go. For the first time in half a millennium, the concept of what is "a book" is changing. With the development of electronic reading devices, the physical object – the medium – of a book can be something other than paper, glue, and ink, while the knowledge and insight contained within is only magnified.

The decline (or, more accurately, the evolution) of libraries and bricks and mortar retailers of books has already begun. Cushing Academy in Ashburnham, MA, a private boarding school my sons attended, has

---

* Horoscopes and Sudoku can be found elsewhere online for free.

already re-envisioned their library for the 21st century. Gone are the stacks and stacks of old books which once gathered dust. Instead, the Fisher-Watkins Library is now all digital. The 20,000 volumes that used to sit on crowded shelves have been removed. No more sets of encyclopedias from the 1970s. No more copies of *Catcher In the Rye* with important pages dog-eared or ripped out. No more dictionaries with all of the swears highlighted. In their place are electronic "portals of civilization," which provide instant access to world-wide dynamic content.

Why have a library with tens of thousands of volumes when you can have one with millions? Why not *billions* of volumes of literature and research available to students? In addition to computer workstations, the library (which partnered with Amazon) offers dozens of Kindle e-readers to students and is poised to adopt any new platforms for the dissemination of content that may emerge. The space that had been taken up by bookshelves has been repurposed as study areas, lounges, quiet areas with noise-cancelling headphones, even a coffee shop for students to gather or relax. Word is, the library at Cushing has never been so full of students and faculty! Ivy League schools such as Princeton are already digitizing their rare books and other holdings and adopting the digital library model as well.

Unlike newspapers, public libraries themselves will not disappear. They too will adopt the newer, more efficient technologies favored by readers. Libraries have been around more than a thousand years before Christ and their primary function was to serve as a repository for all of that culture's works (scrolls, clay tablets, war booty, pamphlets on how to correctly file your taxes). Libraries will continue to exist as lending institutions, but primarily, as archives. They will be the modern repositories of the antiquities we refer to today as "books."

As the publishing model changes and the focus on physical books shifts to electronic versions, the bookstore itself will become an anachronism. The next generation of readers will look back in wonder at why retailers built 100,000 square foot stores to sell books. It's like the way our generation views the local telegraph office or elevator operators.

I know people are very passionate about books. So am I. And I know what the arguments are against the popular adoption of e-readers.

The most specious argument is that it is somehow elitist to suggest that literature be available only to those who can afford a device like a Kindle. That's nonsense. Despite the cost of an mp3 player (and the ancillary computer requirements to operate one), music is still available for mass consumption. In 1900, there were only 600,000 residential telephones in the United States (nearly all owned by the wealthy). Today, according to the CIA World Fact Book, there are 150 million landlines in use in the US and 270 million cellular phones. Less than fifty years ago it was common for whole neighborhoods to gather at the one house that had television in order to see any programming. Today, there are statistically *more* than 1000 televisions per 1000 people in the US. Does anyone really think the price and popularity of the Kindle will not continue to push its mass adoption by readers in the next few years?

But this isn't about what parts of our past we need to preserve. What the students of the future need are not more Barnes & Nobles[*]. They need instant access to content and technology.

Roll 'em

Unlike baseball (which really came from the English game of cricket), hot dogs (which were pressed the first time in Germany), or apple pie (which was originally baked back in ancient Egypt), Hollywood is a genuine American invention. It is through the movie industry that the world sees America and Americans see themselves. The feature film is an art form much appreciated in this culture.

The movie industry and the theaters which show films have often been early adopters of new innovations. Features like Dolby Digital surround sound, IMAX screens, and a renaissance of 3D content are just some examples[†]. These enhancements are so successful that they've been mimicked and adopted in home entertainment (high-definition, 5.1 sound). Movies of the near future will undergo many technological changes, including their distribution methods – such as more digital downloads of films by satellite directly to screens. While many theaters

---

[*] With apologies to Messrs. Barnes and Noble.

[†] The chili cheese nachos, made with a yellowish processed nondairy cheese product, are *not* among the innovations I wish to celebrate.

use this technology today, you can be certain the age of shipping film reels is all but over.

While the technology continues leaping forward, the quality of films being green-lit by the studios remains dubious. The movies being released don't last long in theaters anymore. There seems to be a rush to get them to pay-per-view as soon as the credits are finished rolling. Movies mostly live on in our homes as DVD's or Blu-rays, packaged with bonus features, outtakes, and alternate endings available for viewing at anytime we wish to watch them.

With the experience of watching a film at home being equal to (if not greater than) that of in a theater, why would anyone go? I'll tell you why: *impatience*! Only those who *absolutely must* see the new Bruce Willis action flick the weekend it opens are keeping movie theaters alive. The rest of us can wait until it's on Starz at 8 p.m. on a Sunday night. It's people's own impatience that gets them to pay $10 a ticket to sit behind some kid talking on a cell phone and sit in front of a first-time mother who thought the darkened theater would be the perfect place for her infant to "try" to nap.

IFC, the Independent Film Channel, has started a partnership with indie studios to release new films in video stores and On Demand the same day the films debut in theaters. This saves the studios money on marketing the movie once for the box office, then again for the home viewing market. This is a model that will soon catch on with the rest of cash-conscious Hollywood. Who needs to be impatient when you can either see *Die Hard 5* on your leather couch the very same day you could see it in a candy-encrusted Megaplex surrounded by people text messaging like crazy?

Maintaining radio silence

Radio, as we know it, will not exist for much longer either. People have been digging radio's grave since Uncle Milty first put on a dress, and radio kept surviving only because of programming innovations and emerging technologies. The invention of the transistor in the late 1940s made radios portable. The development of radio formats – in which stations would play only one kind of music instead of many – proved good for business. The advent of the high fidelity FM band gave birth to a new generation of audiophiles. Personal computer technology now allows stations to operate unattended overnight (or around the clock) or simulcast programming from other radio stations or networks. You'd think at this time of unprecedented technological possibilities that radio would again be making a major change to stay relevant. Unfortunately Mr. DJ, they have not.

One of the problems is that the competing technology is so much better than commercial radio. The number of people using radio in the car continues to plummet as iPod usage grows. The sound quality from mp3 players far exceeds radio and its selection and ease of use blow away in-car CD players. The connector for playing and controlling an iPod or mp3 player is the fastest adopted accessory in the automotive industry since the cup tray*.

For those who still like the serendipitous nature of a radio broadcast, satellite radio is slowly draining the life blood of terrestrial radio. Sirius/XM radio's sound quality matches that of a CD's, and the radio device has more functionality – offering on-screen listings of what's playing now on this, and other, stations. Terrestrial radio's counter-insurgency includes a new radio band called "HD radio." It simulcasts conventional FM and AM stations in digital quality. So far, only luxury carmakers like Rolls Royce and Mercedes-Benz have made the new radios standard equipment, while a handful of others offer HD radios as options in their vehicles. Financially, Sirius/XM continues to hemorrhage money (and as of this writing Howard Stern's future with digital radio is uncertain). But as Darwin said, it's survival of "the fittest," not survival of crystal clear reception.

Howard Stern, should he decide to leave satellite radio, will never return to the world of terrestrial radio – with its content restrictions and inability to pay his freight. Maybe his next platform is *totally* digital – maybe an iPhone app?

Ultimately, radio's downfall will be attributed not to technology but to its own outdated business model. The seeds for radio's eventual demise were sown in the 1990s when the FCC deregulated the industry. After the rules were relaxed in 1996, ownership groups started devouring each other, creating mammoth media companies that controlled –

---

*   I don't know this for a fact, but by this point in the book, you're just going to have to go with what I say anyway.

not just individual markets – but the industry itself. Before 1996, no corporation could own more than twenty-eight FM and twenty-eight AM radio stations, and could not own two in the same radio market.* After deregulation, Texas-based Clear Channel Communications, for example, owned and operated approximately 1,200 radio stations, with thousands of employees in hundreds of markets, delivering programming to an estimated 110 million listeners. With an unprecedented amount of operational infrastructure to manage (not to mention billions in debt to leverage), came an awful lot of redundancy. The mega-radio corporations began simulcasting programming and laying off personnel across their *de facto* networks (why pay for a soft rock DJ in Spokane when you're already paying one in Helena to play the same songs). A dozen local radio stations, that for years had been fierce competitors, were suddenly now all working together and broadcasting out of the same building and "combo selling" the rate cards of their new "sister stations." But instead of a dozen DJ's working the midday shift, perhaps one or two live bodies roamed the studio while the rest of the stations were playing pre-recorded tracks or satellite programming[†]. I know a radio engineer who says truthfully of the cluster of stations he operates out of one location, "Today we have more station vehicles in the parking lot than we have employees to drive them."

One guy whom I admire is Howie Carr, the legendary *Boston Herald* columnist and syndicated radio host. Carr started his journalism career in newspaper, a dying medium. He then transitioned into radio, another dying medium. Carr is so self-aware that he freely acknowledges the shortcomings of both these mediums; however, he's been able to maximize the exposure for the benefit of all his endeavors. His radio show creates interest in his newspaper columns, thereby benefiting the *Boston Herald*. His books create interest in his radio show, thereby benefiting Carr's flagship station in Boston, WRKO. His syndicated radio shows bring his content to areas of New England otherwise

---

[*] Under certain circumstances, companies could operate a duopoly if the total listenership for both stations did not exceed fifty percent of the audience.

[†] Want to know if your favorite "local" radio station is live or Memorex? Listen to if the DJ ever gives the local temperature. The weather in Spokane is different than Helena. Also, does the DJ mention the time? It's hard to nail down what time "Stairway to Heaven" ended when you've pre-recorded your back-sell a week in advance.

untouched by the *Herald* and content-starved for "good radio." This synergy benefits all the media outlets he labors in. Most of all, it benefits Howie. I don't know who will be the last radio hosts standing, but I bet Carr is one of them.

Radio's saving grace has always been its local sensibilities. People stuck with their favorite radio station because they could get local weather or traffic reports, local news, and listen in to what local air personalities had to say. Now, the mega-companies have stripped radio of that quality, with very few exceptions, just to keep them on the air. The local content that listeners crave can be found in the blogosphere or on-demand in mobile applications. The only difference between satellite radio and terrestrial radio programming is that satellite radio sounds better (and has few-to-no commercials).

So radio, the Houdini of mass media, tore down its house of bricks and replaced it with very large houses of cost-efficient straw. Now the Big Bad Wolf of digital technology is knocking on the door and breathing hard.

Tube o' plenty

If you think running a radio station is expensive, it's nothing compared to the operational cost of a local television station. We're not talking about dropping a CD into a slot. The facilities, technology, engineering, and production costs required to keep TV signals broadcasting are far more complex. Even if you're doing nothing but running infomercials in Swahili, it costs a lot to stay on the air. And those costs get passed along to – you guessed it – the advertiser.

It has *always* been very expensive to run a TV station, especially one with a relatively rigorous local news operation. It takes many hands to create just one minute of TV content. There are salaries involved in assigning news stories, writing them, shooting them, editing them, and transmitting them from some remote location to the control room – and that's before you add up the salaries of the beautiful people delivering the stories on air. Even the syndicated programming, like Oprah or Ellen, is terribly expensive.

Believe me, television station managers have been looking enviously at radio's relative cost-saving measures and searching for ways to incorporate them. There are now robotic cameras in the studio, off-site master control rooms operating multiple stations, even reporters assigned to multiple stations to give semi-customized content (such as political news from Washington or entertainment news from Hollywood).

Local TV news is no longer local. Nationwide, local staffs are being cut in favor of recycled, canned content. More and more stations have been gobbled up by giant companies who, just as in radio, now control multiple licenses and stations in multiple markets. Getting people to come back to a channel with regularity is key. For nearly two decades, viewers have accepted the quality and convenience of an early 10:00 newscast (usually from independent or nonaffiliated stations), while the affiliates of the Big Three have seen more of their audience hit the hay at 11. The situation in late 2009 was most dire for the NBC affiliates around the country who claimed to have lost thousands of viewers and millions in advertising revenue because their 10:00 lead-in, "The Jay Leno Show," sucked, prompting upheaval in both primetime and late night programming. The bottom line: the local affiliate can't succeed if your network lead-in sucks.

The expense of television will soon be doubled; the ROI on television advertising will soon be halved. As fewer people use their TV's for network programming in favor of noncommercial television platforms and Internet use, the CPM (the cost to reach 1,000 people through that medium) on TV will be impractical for most advertisers. Meantime, the CPM for Internet advertising will remain pennies on the dollar and will provide detailed metrics to prove real ROI.

Mad as hell and not going to take it anymore

At the network level, the days of monster television hits are over. We may see other shows like Seinfeld or Cheers or Friends and ER, but never all on the same night on the same network. That's like hanging out in The Cavern waiting for the next Beatles to appear: it's just not going to happen.

The business model for broadcast television will undergo massive changes. The four major networks are moving toward a subscription-based service. This is because ad revenue alone can no longer support free television. Today's free online television services like Hulu.com and TV.com will eventually be supported by pay-per-view fees or subscriptions. And, yes, all of this will be fully integrated with your Blackberry Curve and your HD plasma.

ABC, NBC, and CBS will program more in the mode of Fox. Primetime will be defined as 8:00 pm to 10:00 pm, instead of to 11:00 pm. The original Big Three are already getting out of kids' programming. Sudsy daytime programming will be next to go.

The traditional television season will no longer start in September and end in May. New series launches are already staggered around the ratings sweeps periods (November, February, and May). No longer needing to pile up a catalogue of 100 episodes required for a syndication deal, broadcast TV series will run for significantly fewer episodes – like the quality cable series do – instead of the usual number of full-season episodes. In the end, this may not only please the network accountants, but also the viewers. The shorter-run series like "Monk," "The Closer," "Battlestar Galactica," and "Mad Men" tend to have fewer "filler episodes." The networks will have to continue the innovations made with "NYPD Blue" and adopt grittier dramas – with more skin and saltier language – to compete with similarly acclaimed shows on premium channels ("The Sopranos," "Sex and the City," "Californication") and standard cable ("The Shield," "Sons of Anarchy," and "Nip/Tuck") where George Carlin's "seven words you can't say on TV" no longer applies.

Interactive all the time

The functionality of computers and the spectacle of HDTV will come together in ways only dreamed of in Ray Bradbury novels[*]. The experimentation with a product by Microsoft's MSN called Web TV several years ago stumbled out of the gate. It was too much, too soon. Had Henry Ford invented the Maserati instead of the Model-T, the first twenty people who drove it would have been killed and we'd all still be riding on horseback. But after years of training, America is ready for interactive TV. As of this writing, Sony and Samsung are bringing new 3D/HD televisions to American living rooms. If you don't want to wear the funny glasses, then Philips, Mitsubishi, and Hitachi are soon

---

[*] And no…I don't mean we'll be burning books like in *Fahrenheit 451*.

to unveil TV sets that render the 3D effect with *your bare eyes!* (Imagine what that will mean for your cat!)

When the astronauts wanted to go to the moon, they didn't just fly there. The early Apollo missions took on critical tasks needed to complete such a mission, like perfecting orbital docking maneuvers, experimenting with spacesuits for use outside of the capsule, and testing different flavors of Tang. Likewise, today's consumers have separately mastered the concepts of emailing, browsing, DVRs, iTunes libraries, mobile uploads, Twitter, and repurposing content for our personal networks. We're now ready to put all these concepts together for a more dynamic and fully integrated entertainment experience.

New technology is emerging to mesh social networking with TV programming, combining the best features of the Internet and the DVR. With Flip cameras shooting in HD, the next generation of YouTube content will look better than homemade, and will be called up on your living room flat screen. Soon, we'll be able – with a click of the remote or a wireless keyboard – to select an alternate ending to a movie.* We'll be able to participate in more significant ways with the programming than ever before. We can give instant feedback on characters and plot twists, and connect with other fans of the show to gossip on cast changes and character hook-ups. Why call an 800 number when you can use your remote to cast a vote for the next American Idol (or the next American President)? Why call into *Regis and Kelly* to answer a "Trivia-a-go-go" question when you can appear via your own living room to blow an embarrassingly easy question about Jude Law that any moron who had actually *watched* yesterday's show would have known that his co-star in *Sherlock Holmes* was Robert Downey Jr.? Not to mention missing out on a chance for you and the person in seat #58 to spend a weekend in the Poconos?

---

* It doesn't have to be as gimmicky as in the 1985 movie *Clue* in which three endings with three different killers was filmed. Virtually any DVD comes with deleted scenes, director's cuts, and alternate endings that are not fully integrated into the programming. You decide! In fact, James Cameron, the creator and director of what is now the highest grossing motion picture of all time, the sci-fi/fantasy drama "Avatar," had indicated that even though the theatrical release of the film ran for 3.2 hours, he still has 45 minutes of additional footage which will be included in a director's cut offered on DVD and Blu-ray.

TV shows themselves will only be extensions of the full entertainment experience for the raving fan. *The Office* has an interactive web presence in which viewers become "employees" of Dunder-Mifflin Infinity, receiving company emails, assignments, and the other humorous drudgery that the sitcom celebrates. Characters of *The Big Bang Theory* are tweeting to followers *in character* about what is happening in their lives. Search for any online content mentioned in *How I Met Your Mother*, and you will find a fully-fleshed out website (TedMosbyIsAJerk.com, canadiansexacts.org), Wikipedia entry (Lorenzo Von Matterhorn)*, or YouTube video (Robin Sparkles in "Let's Go to the Mall").

The section of the industry which has most eagerly adopted the online experience with their shows is children's and teen's programming. The Cartoon Network's live reality show, *The Othersiders*, follows a band of teens who explore haunted places. Their "evidence" is uploaded to their website, where viewers can review it and vote on whether or not the old fort or abandoned hospital is actually haunted. In the Nickelodeon show *iCarly*, the high school-aged main characters run their own webcast; the actual iCarly.com website lives and breathes in cyberspace, offering the same content promised in the TV show, plus submissions from viewers.

So what do advertisers have to do to make themselves relevant in this space? As I said before, they have to give you something in exchange for your most precious commodity: time. That could be a bit of pertinent information or entertainment. But it could also be a chance to participate in the programming itself. Vote for your favorite athlete. Pick the new theme song. Write a new slogan for the product. Advertisers can be the conduit between the audience and the program.

Design-your-own-ads are also very effective. Doritos' "Crash the Super Bowl" contests, in which the best homemade TV ads for Doritos get played during the Big Game, garnered a lot of attention. The NFL even runs contests with fans to pick their favorite "official" ad. One promotion I was a part of featured an online American Idol-type contest in which people sang their own versions of the state lottery's theme song.

---

*   Wikipedia actually deleted this entry created in conjunction with an episode (in which Barney plants a number of fake online articles about his alter-ego, Lorenzo Von Matterhorn, as part of an elaborate pick-up scheme). Despite the quick removal, the phrase "Lorenzo Von Matterhorn" was the number one Google search term for that day.

These kinds of promotions are successful because they are interactive and they allow advertisers to build a database which allows for the deployment of web-based "push pages" of relevant content for a specific consumer demographic.

A more perfect union

Politics and the governance of the people will also be affected by these advances in technology and social media. Voter information and registration will one day soon be available online. Healthy concerns over authentication and fraud possibilities will lead to new innovations in online security, as necessity is the mother of invention. Will you someday cast your vote online or through your TV? Biometric measures, like fingerprints, retinal scans, and facial recognition software, will make that happen. (It certainly would make it more difficult for those committed ACORN volunteers to attempt to steal elections the old-fashioned way!)

Social networking techniques will help politicians mobilize their supporters like never before. As then-Senator Barack Obama demonstrated, the Internet is a great forum through which to collect campaign contributions. The average voter may not want to donate $50 to a candidate, but might be convinced to give $5.00 on ten separate occasions over the course of a campaign season. Most political party machines have an extensive – if not altogether sophisticated – get-out-the-vote effort. Cross tabbing donor/supporter information with potential voting lists can allow neighborhood organizers to cover more ground, even count the number of anticipated votes in a ward before the actual election. They could then contact those folks by email or text several times during the day on Election Day. Poll watchers could gain access to crossed-off voters and those who have yet to show at the local fire station. This voter model process will allow campaigns to monitor their voter turnout models more efficiently, texting, tweeting, and Facebooking those voters who have not yet been crossed off the voter check list.

There is also another efficiency to be gained when office holders utilize social media tools. Think back to those disastrous town hall meetings regarding health care reform that took place in congressional districts across the country in the summer of 2009. Only a handful of people were able to get into the forums and many of them were disruptive activists on both sides. Most of the events turned into donnybrooks with extremists of every stripe jumping in and instigating screaming matches. As we now know, most of the rabble-rousers were ringers – Big Labor activists, insurance industry plants, neo-conservative troglodytes, or socialist malcontents – who weren't even voters in the congressional districts in which the forums were held. It's far too easy to manipulate that kind of forum by stuffing it with a lot of "committed activists."

In the future, more of these "town hall meetings" will be held in cyberspace. Utilizing video chat technologies, representatives can have a nearly unlimited number of participants…but participants would be required to register to demonstrate their residency (and thus their legitimate claims to being a constituent of the public servant holding the meeting). They can be held at regular intervals. There can be strict time requirements, rules of order for participants to follow. It's much harder to disrupt a meeting when someone else can control your volume – or simply shut off your audio and video feed.

Again, for those who fear that it is somehow undemocratic to limit forums with elected officials to people who can afford certain technologies or be blocked from participation due to something objectionable on their sign-in sheet, video town halls need not completely replace live forums. I think it's good for all public officials – local or national, Democrat or Republican – to face the people who elected them. I think it's the elected leaders' obligation to do so. There also has to be a way to leverage the technological tools available to create productive working sessions that make representative democracy more representative, not just noisy.

Ten things you needed to do five years ago

Yes, the world continues to move quickly. If the past ten years have been any indication, the end of the next decade will bring an entirely new paradigm in advertising content and marketing innovation largely driven by technology. Chances are you're already running behind where you need to be now, let alone where you need to be in the future.

Here's a list of things that you, your business, and your advertising people should have been doing all along to stay in step with the "beyond demand" world. And what you need to do now to stay relevant in a braver, newer world ahead.

1. *Terrestrial radio is dead.* If you own a radio station, sell it fast. If you're thinking of buying one, don't. Make sure your new car is satellite radio compatible.

2. *Your cell phone or handheld device will be everything.* Purchase only the latest, greatest model as it's likely to have the processing power for the apps you'll be using in a year (the apps you'll need to use in five years will require a more powerful device than is available today anyway).

3. *Don't bother tipping your paperboy in hope of better services in the future.* There will no longer be home delivery of local papers. Surviving "newspaper" organizations will create one "network" to pool resources and create premium online content which they will need to monetize based on quality.

4. *Store all your books (such as this one) in air tight containers, preserving them for future collectors.* The majority of popular literature will be disseminated electronically. Giant book retailers like Borders and Barnes & Noble will disappear. Those who want hardcopy books or newspapers will get them at specialty stores who print customized content on-demand. Or as always, you will be able to find books from antiquity dealers until the end of time.

5. *Get an HDTV with 3D compatibility and a Blu-ray player.* Movie theaters will slowly fade to black. Why listen to cell phones, obnoxious teenagers, and pay $11.50 for a bucket of popcorn when pay-per-view will continue to be right at home? Independent films already premier on-demand the

same day they're in theaters; soon the studio blockbusters will do the same.

6. *Invest in the modern Marconis.* Wi-Fi or cell phone data access will become universal and a public utility. Consumers can unplug themselves from the radio and TV (to the concern of advertisers) but they want the connectivity which puts the "smart" into their Smartphones. Imagine for a moment you paid for cable TV by the minute; you'd be incredibly selective about what you watched. As long as the meter is running on Smartphone users who are checking email or downloading mobile video, there will be a financial reluctance by the larger public to use their mobile devices as such. Making wireless internet access affordable and ubiquitous will free consumers to use their devices to the fullest – and give marketers access to larger networks of consumers on multiple platforms. Oh and those landlines at home? Unplug them. They are history.

7. *Get a thick skin.* Self-selection of news content will create greater political and cultural rifts among the populace. The political zealots will become more and more like Howard Hughes, taking in content that only re-enforces and rationalizes their own philosophies and beliefs. Bipartisanship, sadly, will be nearly impossible to cultivate as the numbers of entrenched voters who wall themselves off from contrary or challenging views continue to grow. There will be a full third of the population that will never opt-in to hear your political views (either the third that are liberal or the third that are conservative)[*]. The third of the population made up of independent-minded voters may be addressable to you – and that's where the most significant political chess games will be played.

---

[*] I cannot speak yet for the libertarian, vegetarian, or nudist parties, as those databases at least, as of right now, are not quite as robust.

8. *Get a nice profile picture.* Today your network of friends or business contacts may number over a hundred or more. Unlike professional marketers, we don't commonly practice "list hygiene" and purge old names. That guy you talked to twice in high school – and who is now your Facebook friend – is probably going to stay on your list unless he does something stupid to get kicked off, or, unfriended*. And as an ad once explaining why men are not Playboy *readers* but *collectors*, "You're not going to get rid of Miss November just because her month is up?" Over time, our individual social networks, collections of people we've met through the years, will accumulate, yielding several hundreds or thousands of followers.

9. *Enjoy what doesn't suck.* Good news: entertaining, engaging, creative advertising will live to fight another day! TV/streaming video ads will see a resurgence of creativity and cool production with real entertainment value as their aim will be to be shared among social networks and – not just go viral – but go pandemic in their ability to reach the masses.

10. *Get your teeth whitened and get a new stylist.* Interactive TV will get here (in some form soon). No longer will game show contestants be flown in to Burbank. They'll be drawn at random in real-time among the millions of viewers at home. You'll even get your winnings (minus IRS withholdings, of course) automatically credited to your Interactive TV bank account, which you'll be using to instantly purchase the clothes you see your favorite stars wearing or the pizza you suddenly crave during the half-time show.

---

* The word "unfriend" became the 2009 New Oxford American Dictionary's Word of the Year, defined as "to remove someone as a friend on a social networking site," beating out other future classics as "netbook," "hashtag," and "intexticated." There was a brief roil over whether the proper term was "unfriend" or "defriend," but the bickering mysteriously stopped after people on one side of the argument unfriended those on the other.

It's true that our old road of advertising is rapidly aging and the order of media and content delivery is rapidly fading. It's now up to you to look at the rising waters and decide what will happen if you do nothing by just pretending the water will not envelop you and your business.

As Dylan said, "You better start swimming or you'll sink like a stone."

"Come back!" she screamed. "I want to go, too!"
"I can't come back, my dear," called Oz from the basket. "Good-bye!"

The Wonderful Wizard of Oz- L. Frank Baum

Afterword

A lot has happened since this book went to press…

When my collaborator Kevin Flynn and I sat down to discuss writing this book together in June of 2009, we decided to set aside the last chapter to discuss all the developments which occurred since our first outlines. We knew that we'd need some kind of *errata sheet,* something to keep track of all that transpired with the chaotic world of media, advertising, and communications. In other words, we knew our book would be outdated before it was printed.

But that's the point, isn't it? The world is moving too rapidly for any of us to keep up with it. "The wheel's still in spin," as Dylan said. The revolution will not be televised, even if the television is revolutionized.

Here is just a sampling of what's happened in the past few months, further proof that our regular programming will not be seen.

Comcast buys NBC Universal

With a sticker price of $28.2 billion, the country's largest cable company, Comcast, has agreed to purchase a fifty-one percent stake in NBC Universal (NBCU), with a plan to purchase the remaining forty-nine percent from General Electric within seven years. The deal would allow Comcast to promote its cable programming (such as E! Entertainment, PBS Kids Sprout, and the Golf Channel) on NBC's networks (which include CNBC and Bravo), distribute more movies on-demand, and have better control of how cable content is distributed over the Internet. NBC Universal has a library of more than 4,000 movies and 3,000 TV shows, content which is very valuable to a cable provider.

The deal, if it is ultimately blessed by regulators, could give NBCU-Comcast a leg up when it comes to providing relevant content on the Internet and on mobile platforms. Ironically, the National Broadcasting Company was built in the 1930s by David Sarnoff to sell radios for corporate owners GE and RCA, then to sell televisions and then color TV sets. Now, GE is helping broker an ownership deal hoping to move content beyond traditional broadcast channels. If it works (like the way NBC infused revenue into all of RCA's divisions, including its phonograph business), will there be a modern William Paley? He was the owner of the Columbia Phonograph Company and, to beat Sarnoff at his own game, formed CBS.

Déjà-vu, all over again?

In December, AOL (America Online) and Time Warner completed their separation from what the Associated Press labeled "one of the most disastrous business combinations in history."

In the 1990s America Online grew to dominance by providing fledgling home computer users dial-up access to its network and to the Internet. Using $147 billion of its inflated stock, it purchased Time Warner in 2001 hoping to leverage its TV, movie, and magazine content. But as users were attracted to the speed of broadband and DSL, keeping AOL as a $30 a month middleman wasn't an option. Everything AOL offered (news, chat rooms, email, Internet access) could be obtained through other (faster) ISPs. AOL dragged down the company. After nine years of trying to make it work, Time Warner spun off the online content provider.

The independent AOL is now working to re-position itself in the digital world. It acknowledged its failures in customer service and launched an easier-to-use mail product with fewer embedded ads.

Ten is the loneliest number

This section about NBC's ten o'clock experiment – and resulting late night fiasco – had to be written and rewritten several times. The network's bold move to put a variety show block on at 10:00 pm – essentially concede the hour to the other networks – was as troublesome as most critics predicted. "The Jay Leno Show" got about the same number of viewers as "The Tonight Show with Jay Leno" did, but not nearly as many viewers as NBC's traditional line up of 10:00 prime time dramas did. NBC affiliates around the country blamed a ratings sag in their 11:00 newscasts on Leno, saying the 10:00 PM show was a weak lead-in to their telecasts. Now, Leno is back as host of "The Tonight Show," Conan O'Brien gets $45 million while he searches for a new network deal (I'm betting on Fox), and NBC is still in last place.

On paper, the Peacock Network's plan made financial sense. Producing Leno in prime time was still infinitely more cost-effective than producing five expensive one-hour-long scripted dramas (even with the reduced ratings and lost advertising revenue). In the end, the network's inability to stick-to-its-guns and give the 10:00 pm show the full year everyone said would be needed, and their ham-fisted maneuverings to retain both Leno and Conan O'Brien, were far more damaging – financially, artistically, public image-wise – than just running an Indian-head test pattern logo for one hour each night.

Interestingly, the ratings data from that time period suggest something that none of the networks anticipated. It's true that millions of viewers tuned out of NBC at 9:59 pm, but they hadn't been jumping to CBS or ABC (CBS's ratings were down three of the five nights; ABC was down slightly at that hour). Instead, viewers had been using the 10:00 hour to watch programming they pre-recorded on TiVo or their DVR.

This suggests to me something about the way people will use content in the future. While people are statistically watching less television, they seem to be watching more of the television that they love. Life is too short and time is too precious to watch B-grade sitcoms or reruns of crime dramas. With the means and opportunity, viewers will be maximizing the quality of their time in front of the tube, even if they don't increase the quantity of time.

Spins a web any size

Though not as earth-shattering as the NBCU-Comcast deal, the Walt Disney Company has announced it will acquire Marvel Entertainment – the home to Spider-man, the Hulk, and Iron Man – for $4 billion. Disney would acquire the rights to over 5,000 Marvel characters, meaning "Howard the Duck" and "Donald Duck" could soon be making joint appearances at EPCOT.

Go fetch

According to search engine rankings compiled by comScore, Americans conducted nearly 13.6 billion core searches in the month of July. Queries on Google accounting for 64.7% of the search market share. Yahoo came in second with 19.3% of the market. Newly-launched Microsoft site Bing grabbed 8.9% market share. Nearly 4% of searches were conducted on Ask Networks. AOL was used for 3.1% of all Internet searches.

In your face

Facebook continued to lead the way into the digital media frontier. According to Hitwise, the social network site with 300 million members drew 58.59% of all U.S. Internet visits to the top five social sites in September. That was a 194% increase over the same time the previous year. MySpace declined from 55% to 30.26%. Twitter, although up 1,170% from the previous year, made up only two percent of social media visits. Now Twitter is going to leverage its popularity for money, offering advertisers "Promoted Tweets." Time will tell if it will work. For every website that goes from grassroots to business titan (see, *Google*), there are many more that ruin what made them special in the first place (see also, *Napster*).

Meantime, search engine queries for "Facebook" were up 512% in one year, making it the most searched property online. Queries for "Twitter" were up an astounding 1,458% according to Compete. The website reported on its blog that each month more than 65 million users access Facebook through a mobile device. That's nearly a quarter of its users logging on through Smartphones, iPods, and devices other than a PC.

Bigger than the Internet

In a massive report issued by Morgan Stanley, analysts evaluating the industry say that mobile media is poised to become the next great digital platform of the modern era. The report says mobile is ramping up faster than any platform before it and will bring a staggering scale worldwide. As minonline.com described it, "Mobile could well be bigger than the Internet."

Actively interactive

The predictions remain rosy for online advertising. According to a report from BIA/Kelsey, the banner ad market is expected to grow from $897 million in 2008 to $1.9 billion in 2013. Ads that are locally purchased and are deployed to local customers (through geographic-targeting) should grow $45 million in 2008 to $565 million by 2013.

The Forrester Interactive Marketing Forecast reports that sixty percent of media buyers say they intend to increase what they spend on online and social media advertising. They say they'll increase their interactive budgets by cutting back on direct mail, newspapers, and magazines. The report predicts money spent on digital media will near $55 billion in 2014. That's twenty-one percent of all money spent on advertising in the U.S.

In 2008, video ad revenue grew 126% over 2007, to $734 million, according to the Interactive Advertising Bureau. TV ad revenue continues to pull in more than ten times that amount.

Online deployment of commercial video will continue to grow, bolstered by reports such as this: web ads are just as effective as TV ads. The group comScore reported over a twelve-week span, online campaigns involving consumer packaged goods with a forty percent reach of their target segment were responsible for lifting retail sales of the product nine percent, compared to an average lift of eight percent for TV advertising. This kind of research will further bolster the confidence advertisers have about spending money on nontraditional media.

Read all about it

More than 40,000 newspaper jobs vanished in 2009. According to the Bureau of Labor Statistics, there were 284,220 people employed by "newspapers." Ten years earlier, that number was 424,500. In an indication of where journalism is heading, this year the Pulitzer Prize committee accepted entries for web-only news outlets for the first time.

More and more newspapers on life-support pulled the plug in the past few months. The *Rocky Mountain News* in Denver and the *Seattle Post-Intelligencer* both shut down. The *Christian Science Monitor* went to a web-only format.

In a fascinating game of chicken, the *Boston Globe* – and its parent company the *New York Times* - went to the mattresses with the Newspaper Guild seeking $10 million in concessions. The union rejected a salary reduction proposal causing the threats of closure for the city's most prominent paper. At the eleventh hour, the Guild accepted a deal which keeps the newspaper running…for now.

A virtual media war broke out in tiny Claremont, NH which is endemic of the newspaper morass occurring worldwide. When the *Eagle-Times* closed shop in July 2009, it left the small city without a hometown newspaper for the first time in two centuries. Media, like nature, abhors a vacuum. The *Valley News*, published in neighboring Vermont, opened a Claremont office in an attempt to expand their geographic and advertising footprint. At the same time, two new weeklies began operation in town (the *Claremont Compass* and the *Claremont Villager*); two existing weeklies (the *Claremont City Post* and the *Weekly Clarion* in Vermont) beefed up their coverage too. In October, the *Eagle-Times* emerged from bankruptcy and began republishing, meaning there were six papers operating in a city of 15,000.

Since then, one of the new weeklies, the *Claremont Villager*, has folded and sooner or later someone else is going to have to get out of Dodge. In a microcosm I can see how the waning years of the newspaper industry are likely to unfold. Cities that are one-paper towns will systematically become no-paper towns. Newspapers on the geographic outskirts of the coverage area will attempt to establish themselves in the relinquished communities, looking for content and advertisers. Eventually these papers will fail too, leaving larger regions uncovered and presenting opportunities for even larger newspapers to plant their flag. They will become empires which will – like all empires – eventually collapse. Either in the manner of the Romans (collapsing internally under its own debt and deficiencies) or in the manner of the British (over-extending itself, losing influence, and watching its prized properties go independent).

And you thought the *New York Times* had problems.

Rolled up magazines

The number of magazines being published in the U.S. continues to yo-yo. There were significantly more magazines published in 2008 (20,590) than in 1988 (13,541), but this is because new titles come on the market as quickly as failing titles come off. Circulation (our desire for content) remains steady, but advertising revenue has fallen due to the recession.

The Reader's Digest Association filed for Chapter 11 in August after failing to pay a $27 million note due to investors, although operations of the magazine continued. *Playboy* did something it had never done in 60 years of operation: as a cost-saving measure it published a double issue for July & August (yes, there was a double-centerfold). The magazine announced it would publish another double issue for January/February 2010.

Sports Illustrated debuted a prototype of its application for tablet-format devices. Unlike typical static "digital magazines," the SI Tablet's features include a full-screen video clip for a cover shot and an interactive table of contents. The application won high praise from journalists who previewed it. According to them, SI is the first traditional publisher to embrace the full-spectrum of content (video, audio, statistics, etc.) and deploy it in a way that is user-friendly. (Magazine editors have been disappointed with the way their glossy mags render in the black-and-white Kindle.) That's the future of magazines; watch for more titles to embrace content in a format available for reading on mobile devices and eReaders.

I can read you like a book

The market for eReader devices will expand far beyond the Kindle and fragment across many devices. According to Forrester analysts, sales of eBook content will soar to $500 million next year.

In a sign that traditional houses are concerned about how revenue might be lost on hardcover books to virtual ones, the publishers of Sarah Palin's *Going Rogue* and Stephen King's *Under the Dome* decided to not make electronic versions available until after Christmas, forcing the hands of those who wanted to give one as a gift or were too impatient to take advantage of the savings.

Kindle released a version of its eReader for personal computers. Like its iPhone app, it syncs up the library, bookmarks, and notes with the Kindle device. Although it renders book covers in color, magazines deployed to Kindle PC still appear in only black-and-white.

Things got interesting in October when Barnes & Noble introduced the Nook, its response to Amazon's popular Kindle. Unlike the Kindle, it has a color touch screen and the ability to share content with other users. Overwhelming demand for the new eReader made the Nook inventory nearly unavailable for Christmas.

These are not the droids you're looking for

Verizon and Motorola launched the first frontal assault on the iPhone and AT&T by unveiling the Droid. This Smartphone uses Google's Android operating system and comes pre-packaged with a voice-activated version of Google Maps (which will hurt GPS manufacturers like Garmin and TomTom). There are thousands of apps available to download and it can run multiple apps at the same time. The Droid is the first real alternative to the iPhone (for those looking for one).

I believe the growing popularity of the Droid is good for the acceptance of the mobile platform itself. It shows "mobile" is about content and delivery, not the devices. It's not just the "Think Different" Apple cult followers who are driving the demand with their iPhones and iPod Touches. In the way that Pepsi needs Coke, McDonalds needs Burger King, and Batman needs the Joker, these two brands need each other. I don't think Droid and iPhone will cannibalize each other; I think they'll grow the market and raise the stature of the industry.

A fast 18 holes

Who would have thought that squeaky-clean superstar Tiger Woods would have been such a hound? It was revealed Tiger had a larger collection of blonde-haired, long-legged, big-breasted women than Mattel* does.

Aside from the tabloid red meat this marital scandal prompted, it played out as another cautionary tale about the pitfalls of celebrity endorsements. In 2009, *Forbes* magazine reported that Woods was the first athlete to earn one billion dollars in his career, largely due to endorsements. A 2005 ABC News/Washington Post poll found that Woods' had an eighty-five percent favorability rating. A month after the scandal about his extramarital affair broke, Woods' popularity dropped to forty-two percent. Advertisers – who had been trying to leverage Woods' good guy image as much as his championship play – took notice. After taking a wait-and-see approach, Gillette announced it would start to phase out Tiger Woods from future advertising. Consulting firm Accenture dropped Woods, as did watchmaker TAG Heuer. AT&T ended its sponsorship with Woods, but continued to support the PGA event it had sponsored under the golfer's name (AT&T also had its logo on Woods' golf bag; their previous deal gave AT&T the right to use him in advertising but they never got that far).

Among the many lessons of the Tiger Woods sex scandal is that brands always take a chance when they have a celebrity spokesman as the face of their company. It's great for Lowe's when Jimmie Johnson's #48 car wins the Sprint Cup Series. It's not great for Big Red soda when their sponsored driver, Jeremy Mayfield, gets suspended for methamphetamines.

---

* They make Barbie, in case you forgot.

The King is dead, long live the King

It can be argued that the sudden death of Michael Jackson was the first major news story of the Twitter age*. While sitting in my car, I got a text message from CNN saying Jackson was in a coma. Content addict that I am, I then sought out more information on radio, then online and on television.

A great number of people first heard about Jackson's hospitalization through social media and new media tools. So many people around the world began typing the words "Michael Jackson" into Google, Yahoo, and the other major search engines that their protective infrastructures misinterpreted the sudden data surge as a cyber-attack and shut down. Some say Michael Jackson killed the Internet; perhaps not, but it was pretty close.

Like the miracle landing of flight 1549 on the Hudson (in which passengers, rescuers, and spectators alike were all posting real-time information), and quixotic flight of "balloon boy" Falcon Heene (in which tens of thousands of people watched online video and made "balloon boy" the number one search term on Google), our ability to comment on stories in real time is greater than ever. In fact, some media critics wonder aloud if the news drives the social media commentary… or the other way around.

Yes he can?

President Obama's popularity has gone from that of a rock star to that of the Pet Rock. One can argue about the many factors in play, which issues are hurting him. But there are two lessons I've learned from watching and participating in party politics for many years.

One is that, like seemingly everything else in our society, the political pendulum swings much faster now. Technology, the blogosphere, non-stop news, content distributed by any and all media platforms today makes it hard for any modern-day president to keep what he had for

---

* Although the election of President Obama could be rightly argued as a more historically significant event which drew more media coverage, a presidential election is a planned event and hardly breaking news.

lunch a private matter. No longer are voters of our Great Republic content to ride through "eras" like the swing to the left of the 1960s or the swing to the right in the 1980s. Between 2004 and 2010, we've seen the balance of power shift right, left, and coming back to the right again. Consumers of government policy want results *now*. Unlike his predecessors, fewer people are willing to give Obama's presidency the benefit of the doubt. "If *this* doesn't work, let's throw it out and try *something else*." The electorate is more volatile than ever before. Blame Twitter and healthcare reform.

Secondly, there is the problem with the cult of personality and political reality. The expectation bar was placed so high for Obama that he was inevitability going to fail. Now his ideologically pure policies appear to be failing everyone. Independents are now on to him. Even the Democratic base is jumping over the side (remember, it's hard to tell a ship is sinking if all the rats stay on board). Thanks to all the bruising Obama and the Democrats took to pass their so-called "health care reform" bill, things look to be swinging back the Republicans' way. The Tea Party people are energized and 2012 just got that more competitive.

Up the creek without an iPad

In a real stop-the-presses kind of moment, Apple has released its new iPad just as this book goes to the publisher. What does it mean? Well it's too early for us to tell. But it shows us that Apple is thinking ahead to what a personal computing device should be in the future.

There are plenty of questions the new tablet device from Apple raises. What does it mean for e-readers (which have 2x, 3x, or 4x the battery life) and for publishing? What's it mean to netbooks and Microsoft's Slate PC tablet? How is the data package from AT&T going to measure up? Will the average consumer embrace the iPad as their primary entertainment device? Will they do as Apple predicts: dock the iPad all over the house so it can be an alarm clock in the bedroom, a video player in the living room, and a cookbook in the kitchen?

I suspect that you, fair reader, may already know the answer to some of these questions.

There's no place like home

So that brings you up to date…not! As previously stated, this book in its printed form was out of date the second it came off the presses (see iPad above), so here's a little bonus for you. A lot more has happened since this book was published and the moment you got to page 180. And a ton of stuff has happened since you last checked your in-box. Go to this website: www.thatmanbehindthecurtain.com. There, we will continue to provide supplemental information, analysis, and the occasional non sequitur in a footnote too. You can add your comments as well. That means you're reading an interactive book whose relevance will live on long after the copyright date on the title page.

You don't have to be a wizard to survive in the new digital world. But don't be cowardly, don't be stupid, and don't be heartless. Those who have acted that way in today's world of advertising and communication have gotten burned (or worse, melted).

Whether it was nostalgia or patriotism or sexual desire, the best advertising has always been about emotions. Emotions come from connections. If "Reach out and touch someone" can bring a tear to your eye, or "Where's the beef?" can make you laugh out loud, then you've experienced the emotional reaction those advertisers were hoping for. Today, the best way to make a similar connection with potential consumers is not with clever television ads alone. It's with a plan that remains media agnostic and reaches people where they are today: at home, online, and mobile. It's a two-way conversation with people who'll get to know you and your product and hopefully become raving fans.

Once the Great and Powerful Oz revealed his true self to Dorothy and her friends, they all got what they wanted – including the Wizard! So go ahead – don't wait to become the next T-rex! Pull back the curtain and let people see who you and your product – maybe even some day "brand" – really are.

Because advertising is not dead. It's just changing faster than most advertisers are.

Index

A

ABC (American Broadcasting Company) 117, 158, 171, 177
Accenture 177
Acme
 the brand 96
Adams, Mason 115, 116, 117
advertising gland 5, 108, 131
 existance of 5
AIG executives
 fornacation of 65
Alexander, Lamar 134, 135, 136, 137, 138, 139, 140
Ali, Muhammad 41
Alka-Seltzer 22
Allbaugh, Joe 141, 142
Allen, Mel 108
Allen, Tim 67
All Things Considered 88
Altria Group. *See* Philip Morris
Alyson Pitman Giles, 43
AMC (American Movie Classics) 3
American Bandstand 15
American Idol
 audience participation of 15
America (rock band) 1
Am I Hot or Not.com 98
Amtrak 126
Anheuser-Busch 52, 54, 55, 56, 66
AOL 89
Apple 176, 179

Apple, R. W. \"Johnny\"
 interview of George W. Bush 142
A Prairie Home Companion 88
Arbitron ratings 8
Arby's 98
Associated Press 170
AT&T 176
 Tiger Woods sponsorships 109, 177

B

Bailey, Doug 135
Baltimore Examiner 80
Bang & Olufsen 97
Barnum, Phineas Taylor (P.T) 61, 62, 67, 71, 72
Baseball Hall of Fame 98
Batman
 supressed feelings for the Joker 176
Ben & Jerry's 42
Benny, Jack 28, 113
Berle, Milton 21, 153
Bernbach, Bill 28
Berry, Dave 82
Betty
 hotness of 98
beyond demand
 concept of 21
BIA/Kelsey 173
Big Brother
 audience participation of 15
Biggest Loser, The 92

181

Big Mac 39, 125
  quality of 76
Big Red soda 177
BIGresearch 6
Bing 98
Bishop, Mel 112, 114, 115
Blackberry 134
  Curve 105
Black, Charlie 133
Blinkx 6
Blu-ray 9, 22, 87, 153, 163
Body, David 109, 110
Bonfire of the Vanities 25
Boone, Pat
  singing your song 101
Boston Globe 80, 146, 174
Boston Herald 155
Boston Red Sox 98, 120
Bradbury, Ray 158
Brooks Brothers 69
Brooks, Mel 112
Brookstone 42
Brown Simpson, Nicole 119
Brüno 19
Bryant, Kobe 108
Buchanan, Patrick 82, 127, 130, 131, 132, 133, 134, 136, 137, 143
Burger King 98, 123, 176
Burns, Ken 87
Bush, George H.W. 127, 128, 129, 130, 131, 132, 133, 134, 143
  accosted at Bedford Mall 132
  touring Air Force One 129
Bush, George W. 138, 140, 141, 142, 143, 144, 145, 146, 147, 148
  pop quiz of 142
  tobogganing 145
BusinessWeek 47

C

Cabbage Patch Kids 100
Cadbury 115
Cagle, Sandy 57
  Miss February 1982 55, 56
Californication 87, 158

Camels 37
Cameron Coup, William 61
Cameron, James 49, 58, 61, 159
Campbell's Soup 98
Carr, Howie 155
Carroll, Dave
  musical revenge 47
Carson, Johnny 21, 113
Carville, James 131
Casablanca 90
Cavern, The 157
CBS (Columbia Broadcasting System) 158, 170, 171
Chancellor, John 7
Chappelle's Show 87
Chesterfield Supper Club 21
Chevrolet 21
Chia Pet 99
Chicago Sun-Times 80
Christian Science Monitor 174
Chrysler 103
Cincinnati Post 80
Clarke, Arthur C.
  wisdom of 13
Claus, Santa 107
Clinton, Bill 131, 133, 137, 138
clowns 61, 71
CNBC (Consumer News and Business Channel) 92
CNN (Cable News Network) 7, 47, 146, 178
CNN.com 150
Coca-cola 90, 96, 99, 105, 107, 176
  product placement of 91
Coco-Puffs 92
Coen, Robert
  Universal McCann 29
Colgate Comedy Hour 21
Columbia Phonograph Company 170
Compete 172
Consumer Reports 19
Contel Systems 111
Coors beer 100
Corona 91
Cosby, Bill 2

Country Time Lemonade 92
Crest 115
Crosier-Pearson-Mayfield Funeral Home
  connectivity of 20

D

Dancing with the Stars 3
  audience participation of 15
Dante's Inferno 3
Da Vinci Code
  of marketing, existance of 38
  of TV remote controls 76
da Vinci, Leonardo 91
d-Con pest strips 41
Dead Sea salt scrub
  avoidance of 68
Dear Abby 82
DiMaggio, Joe 107
Din, Gunga 88
dinosaurs 78, 93
DirecTV 108
Dodge
  town to get out of 174
Dole, Bob 130, 133, 134, 136, 137, 138
Dole, Elizabeth 138
Dom Pérignon 111
Dove
  percentage of moisturing 22
Draper, Don 3, 10, 25, 29, 31, 35
Droid 89, 176
Dukakis, Michael 122
Dunkin Donuts 53, 54, 102, 105, 107, 111
  iced coffee satisfaction of 16
DVR 6, 21, 25, 29, 76, 85, 86, 87, 90, 91, 92
Dyson 96

E

EA Sports 108
Easy-Bake Oven
  cupcake center consistency of 39
E! Entertainment 169
egress 71
Ellen Show, The 156
email 16, 32, 33, 63, 64, 66, 70, 71, 72, 78, 83, 103, 164, 170
End of Days 80, 86
  for newspapers 81
enfant terrible 145
Entourage 22, 87
Estonia 98
et al
  Latin phrase meaning \ 109

F

Facebook 16, 20, 63, 104, 148
Falcon Crest 86
Family Guy 87
FBI (Federal Bureau of Investigation) 16
Fiji mermaid 71
Flintstone, Fred 21
Forbes, Steve 134, 137
Forrester Interactive Marketing 173
Four Seasons 112, 115
FoxNews.com 150
Fox TV 77, 87, 158
Frederick's of Hollywood 42
Fred's Old Fashioned Onion Dip 5
Frosty Cola. *See* fake stuff

G

Gap, the 103
Garland, Judy 2
Garmin 176
Gatorade 107, 116
General Hospital
  redundancy of 17
Gifford, Frank
  homicidal thoughts of 119
Gifford, Kathy Lee 108
Gillette 109, 177
Gleason, Jackie 107
Glee 87
Going Rogue 176

183

Golf Channel, the 169
Google 18, 41, 82, 98, 160, 172, 176, 178
Gorbachev, Mikhail 108
Gramm, Phil 133, 136
Gregg, Hugh 131, 133
Gregg, Senator Judd 129, 140, 142, 144
Grey Goose 105
Griffin, Sally 120
Griffin York and Krause (GY&K) 58
Gutenberg, Johannes 74, 79

H

Häagen-Dazs 42
Hannah Montana 3
Harper's Bizarre 26
Harris, Andrew 118
Harry Potter
  product placement in 90
Hasbro 108
HBO (Home Box Office) 17, 22, 87, 91
HealthSource 116, 117
Heene, Falcon
  a.k.a. \ 178
Hefner, Hugh 82
Heroes 22
Hershey Chocolate Corporation 41, 98
Hiller, Andy
  pop quizziness of 142
Hingis, Martina 40
History Channel 18
Hit Parade 80
Hitwise 172
Home Depot 67, 68, 69
Hoover 96
Hormel, Jim 109, 110
Huggy Bear
  needing a fix from 83
  waredrobe of 74
Hughes, Karen 140, 141, 142
Hulu 22

I

Iberia
  cheese making in 17
inebriated conventioneer 22
INTERPOL
  sneakiness of 14
iPad xi, 179, 180
iPhone 9, 16, 19, 81, 90, 176, 177
iPod 5, 13, 70, 74, 98, 154, 176
iTunes 22, 87

J

Jack Daniels 105
Jackon, Bo
  what he knows 107
Jackson, Michael 107
  social media coverage of death 178
Jeep 103
Jell-O 101
Jeopardy 15
JetBlue 47
Jeter, Derek 107, 116
Johnson, Jimmie 177
Joker, the 176
Jordon, Michael 108
Jumbo the Elephant 61, 71

K

Kelleher, Herb 45
Kennedy, John F
  Camelot 125
  debates 79
Keyes, Alan 137
Kindle 79, 81, 151, 152, 175, 176
King, Larry 83
King, Rollin 45
King, Stephen 176
Kleenex 98
K-mart 42
  sucks 101
Knievel, Evel
  toy 39
Knocked Up 91

Kool-Aid 101
Kornblut, Anne
  Boston Globe 146
Koslowsky, Bob 55, 56, 57
Kraft
  macaroni & cheese 101
Krause, Elaine 58

L

Late Show, The 48, 108
Laugh-In 29
Law and Order 7, 92
Leach, Robin 109, 110, 111, 112, 113
Legal Sea Foods 118
Letterman, David 48, 77
Levittown
  waking up drunk in 68
list hygiene 66, 165
Little, Rich 112, 113, 114, 115
Longo-White, Rose 58
Lost 91
lottery 21, 58, 70, 109, 110, 111, 115
  player demographics 69
Lottery Replay 69, 70
Lou Grant 115
Lowe's 177
Lucky Strikes 3, 31, 37
Lugosi, Bela 119

M

Madison Avenue 25, 30, 100, 110
  douchey-ness of 11
Mad Men 3
  modern day 25
Maiola, Joel 128, 130, 140, 141, 145, 148
Manning, Archie 108
Manning, Eli 108
Manning, Peyton 108
Marconi, Evelyn 128, 129
market segmentation 61, 62
Marlboro 101
Ma's Convenience Store & Gas Mart 98

Maserati 158
M*A*S*H
  final episode 15
MasterCard 108
Masters of the Universe 34
  not! 25
Matalin, Mary 131
Maverick, Samuel 105
Maxwell House 101
Mayfield, Jeremy 177
McCain, John 139, 141, 142, 143, 146, 147
McDonald's 98, 102, 108, 176
  advertising budget 9
  hospital equivilant of 43
Meat-a-ball
  spicyness of 22
megalomania
  see Karl Rove 148
Miami Herald 80
Michelin 81
micro-segmentation 65
Miller, Glenn
  played songs that made the Hit Parade 80
minonline.com 173
M&M's
  on Air Force One 129
Moxie 120
MP3 70, 74, 152, 154
Mr. Ed 21
Mrs. Fields 100
Mrs. Robinson
  Coo-coo-ca-choo of 64
msnbc.com 150
Murdock, Rupert 82
Murphy, Mike 130, 131, 134, 135, 138, 139, 143, 146, 147
Must-see TV 6
MySpace 33, 63, 78

N

Nash, Gerald 120
National Public Radio (NPR) 88
National Widget Association 26

185

NBC (National Broadcasting Company) 7, 157, 158, 169, 170, 171
Neeleman, David 48
Neiman Marcus 69
New England Revolution 98
newspaper 30, 62, 65, 67, 69, 74, 79, 115, 142, 149, 150, 163
New York Daily News 80
New York Times 19, 142, 174, 175
Nielsen ratings 7, 8
Nike 107, 108
Nip/Tuck 158
Nixon, Richard 79
Nook 176

O

Obama, Barack 143, 148, 161, 178, 179
O'Brien, Conan 171
Ogilvy, David 28
Old Lady Channel
  hypothetical existence of 18
Old Navy 90
O'Neil, Gary 51, 57
O'Neil Griffin and Associates 57
O'Neill, Thomas Phillip \ 133
Oprah 156
Oreo 108
Oscar Meyer 101
Oyster, Duffy 53, 54
Oz 1, 2, 141, 180

P

Paley, William 170
Palin, Sarah 176
  blog? 150
PBS Kids Sprout 169
PBS (Public Broadcasting System) 87, 169
Pepsi-Cola 92, 96, 107, 125, 176
PerezHilton.com 150
Pete Rose 98
Pet Rock 178
Phelps, Michael 108

Philbin, Regis 108
Philip Morris 101
Pick Three, LTD 109, 110
Pizza Hut 57, 108
Planter's mixed nuts 92
Playboy 55, 56, 57, 82, 165
Pocahontas 23
Polar Beverages 96
Politico 150
Pollyanna 147
Pony Express 81
Pope
  selection of 97
Pottery Barn 42
Powell, Colin 134
Powerade 108
Procter & Gamble 103
Proulx, Gloria 58
Puffs 98

Q

Q factor 96
Quaker Instant Oatmeal 92
Quayle, Dan 128, 138

R

Rasputin 148
Rath, Tom 134
Reader's Digest Association 175
Reagan, Ronald 114, 134
  Morning in America 125
Red Lobster 43
Rescue Me 3, 91
Restoration Hardware 42
Ripa, Kelly 108
Rivera, Geraldo
  expulsion of 20
Rocky Mountain News 80, 174
Rolex 105
Rotten Tomatoes 19
Rove, Karl 140, 141, 142, 143, 146, 147, 148
Ruzzito, Phil
  for the Money Store 108

S

Samuel Adams 91
San Francisco Chronicle 80
Sanka 102
Sarnoff, David 170
Schwarzenegger, Arnold 113, 114
Sears 42, 120
Seattle Post-Intelligencer 174
Seinfeld 98
Sex and the City 158
Shakespeare, William
  apologies to 110
Sharper Image 42
Shasta 96
Shecky's Matzo Ball Noodle Soup 98
Sheehan, Grace 58
Shield, The 3, 158
Shore, Dinah 21
Showtime 17, 87
Simpson, OJ 119
Simpsons, The 76, 87
Sir Galahad 2
Sirius/XM satellite radio 22, 77, 82, 154
Slate 150
Slate PC 179
Smartphones 19, 76, 83
Smelly Cat
  song 6
Smucker's 116
  it has to be good 115, 116
Snuggie 39, 99
Sons of Anarchy 158
Sopranos, The 22, 141, 158
South Dakota
  relative size of 18
Southwest Airlines 45, 46
Spielberg, Steven 49, 58, 59
Sports Illustrated 175
Spot the Wonder Dog 29
Sprint 108
Starbucks 20, 98, 101, 102, 105
Starz
  Bruce Willis on 153

Stern, Howard 82, 154
Stevens, Darrin 32, 34
Stewart, Jimmy 114
Styrofoam 39, 105
Sullivan, Ed 21
Super Bowl 7
  ratings of 7
  trips to 55
Svengali 148
Sweet Baby Ray's 104
Synovate 86

T

Taco Bell 103
TAG Heuer 109, 177
Tamposi, Sam 120, 121
Tang 159
TD Bank 108
Teeter, Bob 130
Television Bureau of Advertising 7
Texaco Star Theater 21
Texas Death Stare 145
Thumb, General Tom 71
Tickle-Me Elmo 100
Time magazine 19, 80
Timex 105
Titanic 58
Toast of the Town 21
TomTom 176
Tonight Show, The 8, 21, 114
Tranchemontage, Scott 144
Treaty of Ghent 20
T-rex 78, 180
Tri-State Lottery 109, 110, 117
TV Guide 17
Twitter 19, 33, 83, 159, 172, 178
  tweets 16, 41, 48, 78, 83, 104

U

Under the Dome 176
United Airlines
  breaks guitars 47

V

Valdez, Juan
  coffee envy of 102
Van Dyke, Jerry 117, 118, 119
VCR 21, 28, 76, 85, 86
verisimilitude
  author's showy use of the word 38
Veronica
  hotness of 98
Viagra 4
Vick, Michael 108
Victoria's Secret 42
Videoscan 87
Virginia Slims 101
von Bülow, Claus
  lack of celebrity endorsement opportunities for 41

W

Walmart 67, 68, 69, 98
  as country store 67
  internal culture of 42
  shopper profile 69
Walt Disney World 89
Wayne, John 121
Welch, Ted 134
Wi-Fi 20, 101, 164
Wilbur Chocolate 98
Williams, Ted 120, 121, 122, 123, 124
Wilson, Pete 134
Winstons
  smoked by Fred Flintstone 21
Wolfe, Tom 25
Wonder Bread 97
Woods, Tiger 109, 177
World Widget Expo
  in Greenland 26
WRKO 155

Y

Yahoo 172, 178
Yawkey, Jean 121
Yawkey, Tom 121

YouTube 47, 79, 91, 104, 159, 160

Z

ZAGAT 19
Zune 98

Patrick Griffin is a longtime New England ad man. He has won numerous awards for creative advertising in print and broadcast. He is also the premiere political consultant for the first-in-the-nation New Hampshire presidential primary. He is chairman of Griffin York & Krause, a marketing innovation company. Pat is a scratch golfer, former Olympic tri-athlete, and a Nobel Prize recipient*.

For more information, go to www.thatmanbehindthecurtain.com

---

*   Not actually true, but it makes for a better bio. In advertising this is known as overstating the product's benefit.